Earl
by Betty Lauder '97

This book, *Why Are There More Horse's Asses Than Horses*, was published by Kindle Direct Publishing in 2023, and additional copies of the book can be purchased on Amazon. The book is available as either a hardback or paperback publication.

DEDICATION

Earl and June were high school sweethearts and married in 1942, at the ages of nineteen and eighteen years, respectively. In total they were married seventy-six years, which Earl would say is a world record for a bartender.

This book is dedicated to Earl's wife June who throughout those seventy-six years put up with Earl's drinking, smoking, gambling, and late nights away from home, and all the late nights away from home that turned into early mornings away from home.

Earl and June

The dedication is also extended to any and all bartenders that have been married more than seventy-six years, if and only if they or their families can supply undeniable proof that they were married for that long.

TABLE OF CONTENTS

                                                                              Page

DEDICATION..3
ACKNOWLEDGMENTS..6
REQUEST FOR ADDITIONAL STORIES........................8
INTRODUCTION..9
CHAPTER 1..15
    TALES FROM EARL'S BARS..................................15
CHAPTER 2..37
    EARL AND HIS FRIENDS.......................................37
CHAPTER 3..58
    EARL AND HIS FAMILY..58
CHAPTER 4..79
    EARL'S JOKES...79
    Bartending and Drinking...................................79
    Health...86
    Money..87
    Old Age...89
    Wife and Marriage..91
    Sports...94
    Sex..95
    Questions...99
    Other..100
CHAPTER 5..103
    EARL'S ADVICE..103
EARL'S NOTES...111

LIST OF PICTURES

	Page
Earl and June	3
Earl with His Mom and Dad	9
Earl as a Salvation Army Basketball Player	10
Earl and June Newly Married	11
Earl and June with Their Children	14
The Olympia Cocktail Lounge	17
Earl's Wooden Native Statue	28
The Trade Winds Bar	32
The Tunnel Bar	33
Earl Kisses Bud Biddle While Bud's Wife Watches	38
Norm Held at Earl's Cigar and Coffee Shop	40
Andrew Briggs and Earl	42
Earl as a Child Playing with Something in His Pocket	43
Earl with Jim Melson and Bill Sebree	45
Newspaper Advertisement for Earl's Birthday	48
Earl Kissing Linda Davis While Jeff Harden Poses	54
Farewell Toast to Earl at His Gravesite	56
Earl with His Daughter Susie Erehart	60
Earl with His Sons	64
Dave Alger in the MG	65
Earl Admiring Marianne Bergamo's Figure	67
Earl's Happy Birthday Sign	71
Earl and June Waving Goodbye	110

ACKNOWLEDGMENTS

On behalf of my father, I would like to thank the following friends of Earl's that supplied stories for this book or have been mentioned in the book. In alphabetical order they are Keith Alfrey, Earl Allen, James "Jim" Anderson, Bill Ballard, Modie Beeman, Robert "Bob" Begley, Darin Benson, Max Benson, Melvin "Bud" Biddle, Tim Brandon, Andrew "Andy" Briggs, Rhonda Briggs, Ron Bryson, Lorrie Bryson, Tom Bushey, Leo Campbell, Tim Carpenter, Shannon Chambers, Sue Clayton, Bill Collins, Ward Collins, Duane Cox, Doug Davis, Ward Davis, Jerry Duncan, Dick Dunn, Jerry Fuller, Opel Gilliam, Bernie Glazer, Melda Goodman, Martha Baker Green, George Griswold, Jeff Hardin, Ed Hedgecraft, Norm Held, Jim "Bird" Hiatt, Phillip Hoose, Donald "Don" Hunter, Dave Imel, Paddy Jamerson, Leann Jones, Jonesy, Glenn Keeney, Rick Kellams, Betty Lawler, Earl Lawson, Monty McCune, James "Jim" Melson, Bob Mullins, Jim Neely, Joe Peoples, Donald Phillippe, Bill Pitts, Ron Porter, Virldeen Redmon, Bill Rodgers, William "Bill" Sebree, Leonard Sharp, John Gordon Smith, Dan Spall, Erick Spencer, Fredrick "Fred" Spencer, Mark Szalaiy, John "J.T." Thomas, Gary Timmons, Pug Vaughn, Ed Ward, Bill Wallace, and Don Wood.

For the most part, the jokes and stories in this book came from Earl's notes. Unfortunately, I was unable to interpret all of dad's notes, hence stories involving the following people could not be included in the book: Bob Church, Ron Clark, Jim Ditzen, Bill Fleiman, Paul Green, Jerry Hite, Kate Hockama, Tom Hockama, Vic Kellum, H. Lumford, Joe Eddie Miller, George Rambo, Harry Taylor, and Jack Tilley.

Dad's family must also be thanked for their love and stories, and that includes his father Frank Alger; mother Mable Alger; sister Betty Chambers; wife June Alger; mother-in-law Ruby Simpson; sons Dave, Dean and Doug Alger; daughter Susan Erehart; son-in-law Steve Erehart; daughters-in-law Laura Alger and Marianne Bergamo; and grandchildren Andy Alger, Katy Pearson, Matt Helpling, Lauren Pratt, Patrick Alger, Connor "Max" Alger, Abby Rivers, Sam Erehart, and Emma Erehart.

Betty Lawler, Earl's sister-in-law, deserves special recognition for the caricature of dad used at the front of this book. Further, a story in the book mentions Betty and her daughter's family, more specifically Jean Zaiser, her husband Breck, and children Jordon and Luke. Tom Taylor and his sister Martha Borman, Earl and June's nephew and niece, also supplied stories.

Lastly, it is decidedly proper to thank all of Earl's wonderful friends and customers, whether or not they were mentioned in this book. Earl loved you all, and enjoyed making you smile and laugh and forget about your troubles even if it was just briefly.

Dean Alger

REQUEST FOR ADDITIONAL STORIES

There are likely a significant number of fascinating stories about Earl or Earl's bars that the family has never heard, or has forgotten, and therefore could not be included in this book. If you want to share other stories, please email them to Dean Alger at algerindy@gmail.com. Maybe we will receive enough stories to create volume two of this book.

INTRODUCTION

Earl often joked that he wanted to write a book, but he had to wait until everyone died. He also said he was going to name the book, *Why Are There More Horse's Asses Than Horses*. The family laughed every time we heard this, and we thought he was joking. After he died however, we found an envelope with scraps of paper containing his hand-written jokes and thoughts. So it looks like Earl really did want to write this book, and here it is, Earl's stories, jokes, and advice, with contributions from his family and friends.

Earl with His Mom and Dad (left to right Earl, Mabel, and Frank)

Earl was born at home, 428 West 4th Street in Anderson, Indiana, on Friday August 31, 1923. His parents were Frank and Mabel Alger. Frank worked primarily as an electrician at Delco Remy and Mabel was a homemaker. Earl's sister Betty was six years old when he was born, and Earl adored her and she him. When talking about Betty, Earl would often mention that she bought him his first bicycle when she started working after high school. Earl grew up during the Great Depression, he was about six years old at the start of the depression and sixteen when it ended. His family, like most families at this time, did not have much money. Earl always said, "Everyone was poor but didn't know it." He also remembered eating a lot of fried beef liver and onions because liver was cheap.

Earl had many childhood friends that would stop in his bars, and they said Earl could do most anything that kids thought were important, such as climbing the highest tree or hitting the most basketball free throws. They may have been right as the family has a newspaper clipping showing Earl won the city of Anderson marble tournament when he was a kid.

Earl as a Salvation Army Basketball Player

In 1941 Earl graduated from Anderson High School. His wife and children have heard stories that Earl was kicked off of the Anderson Indian's basketball team his freshman year for smoking, although this may just be part of the mystery and lore that surrounds Earl and his life. We do know that he played basketball well into his thirties on various amateur teams, including two state championship teams.

Earl and June Newly Married

He married his high school sweetheart June Simpson at the age of nineteen, June was eighteen years old. They started dating after he pulled up in his father's car and asked June and two of her friends if they wanted rides home. June got in the car and the others decided to walk home. Leo Campbell was asleep in the backseat of the car, so they took him home before heading to June's house. They talked and listened to music in the car, outside of June's house, until June's mother flicked the porch light off and on. June told Earl that she had to go inside, and Earl kissed her. That was how their relationship started and they were married seventy-six years. June was likely surprised at times that the marriage lasted so long, as more than once she put his clothes on the front porch when he came home late, after closing the bar, because he was drinking and gambling.

After December 7th, the day Japan attacked Pearl Harbor, Earl received his military draft notice. He was inducted into the Army Air Corp at Fort Benjamin Harrison, in Lawrence, Indiana along with his childhood friend Ward Collins. They rode together on the train to Fort Benjamin Harrison. Earl completed his basic training in Miami Beach, Florida staying in a fancy hotel on Collins Avenue, and marching on the white, sandy beaches. Earl would tell people that marching in the sand was horrible. He ended up working on airplane blind landing devices and because of this skill he never left the United States, spending most of his time at airbases in Florida and Georgia. He was really disappointed that he did not get an opportunity to serve overseas in combat.

Earl was a bartender and bar owner for over fifty years. A job he enjoyed and thrived at. He owned and bartended at many drinking establishments during his career, and even in his nineties he could name every one of them. It was quite an extensive list, and he would name the bars quickly in a rapper-like way. He also supplemented his bar income with gambling, playing high-stakes gin rummy. People came from all over to gamble with Earl, and he would play gin games with them in the bar while he also made and served drinks to customers. Crowds would sometimes gather to watch Earl's card games, especially if the stakes reached $1,000 per hand or more. Earl was a skilled gambler and won a lot of money doing so. When asked how he won so much, Earl would laugh and reply, "I'm lucky and I cheat."

Before bartending Earl worked as a short order cook, Pepsi Cola delivery person, beer distributor, and shuffleboard salesman. And for a brief time he was a factory worker at Delco Remy, a job he hated so that didn't last long. Between bartending jobs Earl even sold Fuller Brush products, and later in life he owned and ran a coffee and cigar shop which his son Dave helped him start.

Along the way Earl and June had four children, Dave is the oldest, Dean as Earl would say is the number two son, Susie the only girl, and Doug the youngest. They raised their children in north Anderson, buying a small three bedroom and one bath house in the late 1950s. The house was physically crowded and full of love. Earl lived in this house until he died on December 1, 2018, and June at age 99 still lives there, on her own, missing Earl. Earl was immensely proud of his children, and he would brag about them. He told anyone who would listen that his kids are all college graduates, Dave an attorney, Dean a geologist, Susie a nurse, and Doug a businessman.

Earl had a unique ability to befriend people. He genuinely loved people of all types and enjoyed spending time with them. He never judged anyone. He also helped people in need by supplying advice, encouragement, and money. But most important, he made people smile and laugh when that is what they really needed.

Dean Alger

Earl and June with Their Children (seated Earl; standing left to right Doug, Susie, Dean, June, and Dave)

CHAPTER 1
TALES FROM EARL'S BARS

Earl would say, "I know all the thieves and troublemakers." He also knew all the movers and shakers in Anderson, Indiana. When you walked into one of Earl's bars, or the coffee and cigar shop he owned, you might see Indiana Supreme Court Justice Donald "Don" Hunter, Judge James "Jim" Melson, Judge Fredrick "Fred" Spencer, Attorney David "Dave" Alger, Attorney James "Jim" Anderson, State Representative William "Bill" Sebree, Police Chief Paddy Jamerson, Anderson High School Basketball Coach Norm Held, and many others.

🍺 🍺 🍺

Justice Donald Hunter, of the Indiana Supreme Court, typically stopped by Earl's bar daily. As he walked in the bar, he always called out, "Earl, I suppose it's your birthday let's have a drink."

🍺 🍺 🍺

At Earl's Tunnel Bar there was no parking lot, so customers parked on the street. The Tunnel Bar was also directly behind the Madison County Jail, and police officers would routinely drive past the bar at all hours of the day and night. A uniformed police officer walked into the bar one night and told Earl there were cars out front illegally parked. He also told Earl he wanted the cars moved. Earl responded, "I can't move them. You'll have to talk to my customers." He then pointed out the various judges, attorneys, and public figures in the bar that the police officer should talk to. The officer without saying a word immediately turned away and walked out of the bar.

🍺 🍺 🍺

While talking about his good friend Judge Fredrick "Fred" Spencer, Earl would say, "If I have to go to court, I want the judge to know my name."

🍺 🍺 🍺

Earl was friends with many police officers in Anderson, Indiana and they often visited Earl at his various bars. At Shannon's Bar, a police car would occasionally pull up outside, and Earl would have his waitress take drinks out to the officers. According to Darin Benson, Earl sent a few drinks to his dad, Officer Max Benson, this way.

🍺 🍺 🍺

A uniformed police officer from the Anderson Police Department stopped in the Olympia Cocktail Lounge (also known as the Olympia Lounge or Big O) and asked Earl for a beer to go. Earl was busy making drinks for other customers and it was taking a while to get to the officer's beer, so the police officer yelled out that he needed his beer now. Earl at once stopped what he was doing, and grabbed a beer can and opened it. He then poured the beer into a paper bag and gave the officer the beer-soaked bag.

🍺 🍺 🍺

New Olympia Cocktail Lounge Is City's Finest

Martin L. Carpenter, owner of Olympia Lanes, Inc., 1312 W. 29th St., announces the opening of the new Olympia Cocktail Lounge. joy bowling and who have expressed a desire for added entertainment and refreshment. Salesmen and business men are The establishment and management extends sincere invitation to all bowling enthusiasts to patronize the Olympia Bowlin

The Olympia Cocktail Lounge (Earl bartended here for many years)

🍺 🍺 🍺

As you can tell from these stories Earl had a great relationship with the local police force. He also got to know and was respected by officers with the Indiana State Excise Police, the agency that enforces Indiana's alcohol and tobacco laws at bars. One of these officers definitely liked Earl, as he stopped at the Olympia Cocktail Lounge just to tell Earl that he knew his story (he knew Earl gambled at the bar) and he was going to leave and let him stay open.

🍺 🍺 🍺

When Earl owned the Stables Nite Club in the mid-1960s, Earl's son David would stop by the bar after school to borrow the family car. Dave was sixteen at the time. Earl once asked Dave to come in and have a seat at the bar. This was quite unexpected as Earl had never let any of his underage children in the bar during working hours. He then asked Dave what he wanted to drink. Dave said a Coke, and Earl responded that he knew Dave drank beer because he had found the beer cans in the car. Next Earl said, "Come on, don't you want a beer?" Dave said, "Ok, I'll have a Pabst Blue Ribbon." Earl opened a beer, placed it in front of Dave and told him, "Before you take a drink let me introduce you to the guy beside you. His name is Pug Vaughn and he's a police officer in charge of the juvenile division."

Earl would say, "The Stables had nine sleeping rooms, nine baths, and no rent from these rooms." June was always upset that Earl never rented any of the rooms above the bar, and instead let people stay and sleep there for free. One of the people that stayed there for free, Earl Allen, was an older, semi-homeless guy that Earl hired to clean up the bar.

There were multiple newspaper articles on Earl and his life. In one of these articles Earl was quoted as saying, "You meet the nicest people in a bar, and you meet a few fools."

Earl was extremely protective of his customer's privacy. When answering the bar phone and finding out someone wanted to speak to a customer, Earl would yell out the customer's name and let them decide if they wanted to take the phone call. Sometimes the customer was right in front of Earl and refused to take the call.

🍺 🍺 🍺

Numerous wild characters came to Earl's bars to visit him. Earl's friend Ed Hedgecraft brought his dog to the bar, and before the night was over Ed was buying shots for himself and the dog.

🍺 🍺 🍺

Monty McCune, a customer and friend of Earl's, was a professional boxer. Earl said Monty lost his last twenty-seven fights and ended up in a nursing home for eleven years, with dementia, from all the punches he took.

🍺 🍺 🍺

Don Woods told people that he was a doctor, although his friends and family knew better. At the Olympia Lounge, Earl's wife June walked in the back storage room and saw Don Woods and the waitress in a compromising situation. The waitress was topless, and Don had a hand under each bare breast. As he moved her breasts up and down, he said, "You're right…one is a little bigger than the other." June later had to explain to the waitress that Don was not a real doctor.

🍺 🍺 🍺

Ed Ward at Earl's bar would say, "I am ok with you odd people." Earl would then tell his customers, "Every day at work I feel the same way as Ed…until I have my first drink."

🍺 🍺 🍺

Earl saw the book *Hoosiers*, on Indiana high school basketball, at a local grocery store. As Earl picked up the book to look at it, a friend walked by and asked Earl if he was going to buy it. Earl responded, "only if my name is in it." Unknown to Earl his name was in the first sentence in the first chapter of the book. Earl bought the book upon seeing his name.

🍺 🍺 🍺

Anderson, Indiana for over fifty years was a hotbed for high school basketball. At its peak in the 1980s, the Anderson High School Indians had a gymnasium, the Wigwam, which seated 9,000 people and routinely sold-out for basketball games. This was an amazing feat for a town with a population of 65,000 residents. Ron Porter, an avid Indians basketball fan and long-time friend of Earl's, had moved to Houston, Texas and really missed the Indians ball games. So if Ron really needed a hometown basketball fix, he would call Earl at the bar when the Indians were playing, and Earl would place the receiver against the radio so Ron could hear the game. Phillip M. Hoose used this story at the start of chapter one in his book *Hoosiers*.

🍺 🍺 🍺

Earl's customer and friend Tom Bushey was a large man who owned used car lots in Anderson, Indiana. Tom's marketing slogan for his car lots was that he was, "The round man with a square deal."

🍺 🍺 🍺

As soon as Tom Bushey walked into Earl's bar, Earl would say, "Oh no, not Tom. Don't you dare Tom, don't do it." Tom would then, after making sure music was playing on the juke box, do a short dance, suck in his stomach, and his pants would fall down.

🍺 🍺 🍺

If someone mentioned Tom Bushey or some of the peculiar things that people did at the bar Earl would say, "I hated to see them until I had a couple of drinks, then it was ok."

🍺 🍺 🍺

Tom Bushey always said his mom was a floosy, and she dated Al Capone when he visited the Green Lantern bar and dance hall outside of Anderson, Indiana. He would tell people he was Al Capone's son.

🍺 🍺 🍺

At the Tunnel Bar Earl told his waitress, Sue Clayton, who dated a lot of men, to take a day off and get some strange. Sue ended up being gone for three days and disclosed to Earl that she had to go all the way to Indianapolis to find some strange stuff.

🍺 🍺 🍺

A customer at the Olympia Lounge, Jim Neely, worked nights across the street at Guide Corporation. On workdays Jim would clock in at the factory, then immediately go to the Olympia Lounge where he would drink and socialize for eight hours. At the end of his work shift Jim would return to the factory to clock out. Earl, who usually worked twelve hours a day and rarely missed work, saw Jim's work habits, and wondered how he kept his job without getting fired. When the plant superintendent stopped at the Olympia Lounge for drinks, Earl asked him why Jim got paid for drinking all night. The superintendent said Jim was the union steward, and they would rather pay him to drink at your bar than have him in the factory causing trouble. Upon Jim's retirement, Guide Corporation could not find any work records showing where Jim worked, what he did at work, and who he worked for.

🍺 🍺 🍺

A married customer of Earl's, who was a superintendent at Guide Corporation, started dating one of Earl's waitresses. After they had been seeing each other for a while, and on a night when she wasn't working at the bar, the waitress came running into the Olympia Lounge looking for Earl. She said she had driven across town to get Earl's help, and she couldn't wake up the superintendent boyfriend who was unconscious in the front seat of the car. Earl hurried to the car and quickly realized that the guy was dead. Earl knew the waitress well. He was friends with the guy that had died. He was also friends with the guy's wife, who had no idea that her husband was cheating.

🍺 🍺 🍺

Earl drove an Isette-Vespa bubble car when he owned the Stables Nite Club. The car was somewhat egg shaped with an engine in the back and bench seat in the front. There was a canvas covered sunroof, and the entire front of the car opened up for access to the bench seat. The vehicle weighed about 815 pounds, so it was quite small. One night after closing the bar, Earl walked out of the building and his car was gone. He later found it across the street on the courthouse lawn, balanced on top of a utility pole guidewire. Four of his friends had physically picked up the car and carried it on to the courthouse lawn.

🍺 🍺 🍺

Bernie Glazer was a childhood friend of Earl's who spent a lot of time in Earl's bars. He was a well-known local businessman and part owner of Glazer Brothers, a scrap metal business. Bernie explaining why he was financially successful would say, "I operate on small margins, buying scrap metal for fifty percent or less of its value and selling it for ninety percent or more." When Bernie was drinking, however, he often reversed these two percentages leaving people perplexed or laughing.

🍺 🍺 🍺

After an evening of drinking with Earl at the bar, Bernie Glazer was going to be late getting home to his wife. This was not the first time Bernie didn't make it home on time because of his drinking, so Bernie knew his wife was going to be exceptionally mad. He thus asked Earl to call his wife and patch things up, or at least soften her attitude somewhat before he headed home. As Earl started to make the call, Bernie stopped Earl from dialing the number and started telling Earl what to say and how to say it. This went on for quite some time with Bernie constantly changing his mind on what needed to be repeated. Earl as the known local jokester of course told everyone this story and would even say, "Bernie was late getting home and wanted to help me call his wife."

After they saw one of Earl's waitresses make a silly mistake, Earl told the female customer he was talking to that he had a low tolerance for stupidity. The customer responded, "Why thank you Earl."

Margie was an elderly lady that owned and ran a brothel in Anderson, Indiana. On the rare occasion when Margie ran out of beer for her customers, she would telephone Earl and ask him to bring over a few cases. Because Earl enjoyed talking to Margie, he often ended up selling beer to her for twenty-five cents a bottle and buying it back for a dollar per bottle while they chatted. After closing the bar once, Earl delivered beer to Margie and didn't make it home until 6 A.M as he was talking with Margie. When Earl explained to his wife June why he was out all night, June kicked him out of the house, slamming and locking the door in his face.

One of Earl's friends asked to borrow a hundred dollars to get his wife out of jail. Earl told him that was a lot of money and asked how much money he had in his wallet. The friend said eighty dollars. In response Earl said, "It sounds like you only need twenty dollars." The fellow than said, "But Earl, that's my beer money."

🍺 🍺 🍺

One of Earl's customers was letting his change pile up on the bar in front of him. After the stack of money got quite large, Earl picked up a quarter and told the guy it was for the juke box. The customer, irritated by Earl taking the quarter, responded that he wasn't listening to music, and he wanted his money back. Earl gave him the quarter but later walked over, picked up another quarter, and said, "You were tapping your foot."

🍺 🍺 🍺

A first-time customer came into Earl's establishment and took a seat at the bar. He stayed in that seat for eight hours, drinking many beers, not going to the bathroom, and not talking to anyone. As Earl was curious, he made sure to watch the guy as he left the bar and walked to the parking lot, where the man unzipped his pants. Earl quickly ran out to the parking lot and informed the guy he couldn't pee there. The guy with a confused expression on his face said, "I'm not going to." And he pointed a finger the opposite direction and said, " I'm going to pee way over there."

🍺 🍺 🍺

Gary Timmons was drinking at Earl's Tunnel Bar when a guy came in that could barely walk. Earl and Gary both noticed how drunk the guy was and Earl said, "It's a good thing he's driving…because he's too drunk to walk."

Earl would occasionally loan customers money if they provided him with some type of collateral, such as a watch or ring. So when a customer that Earl didn't know very well ran out of money but still wanted a six pack of beer to-go, Earl joked that the guy could have a six pack only if he removed his shoes and socks and put them in the beer cooler. Earl said he would return the shoes and socks when the guy paid for the beer. Surprisingly, the guy liked and agreed to this outlandish deal, and he went home barefoot with a six pack of beer under his arm.

If you drank too much at one of Earl's bars you might soon regret, it. Earl had a customer one evening that passed out at the bar, so Earl called a cab and sent the drunk to Jonesy's bar with a note penned to his shirt telling Jonesy to take care of him. Jonesy was another well-known bartender in Anderson and a friend of Earl's. This started a crazy trend, and both Earl and Jonesy would send drunks to each other's bars this way.

When another customer passed out at Earl's bar, Earl had a friend pick the guy up in a hearse and take him to a local funeral home. The drunk must have been surprised and even shocked upon finally waking up, whether it was inside the hearse or the funeral home.

🍺 🍺 🍺

"Cherry brandy for me and my friends," was a common announcement that Earl would make at his bars. When everyone that wanted a shot of brandy had one in hand, Earl would propose a toast. He usually had the men drink to pussy, booze, and hillbilly music, and the women drink to peter and bubble gum. No one really liked the cherry brandy; they did however enjoy toasting with Earl. Earl would joke that they were drinking cherry brandy, because it was the only liquor that the bar did not inventory.

🍺 🍺 🍺

Earl and June decided to take a trip to Hawaii to visit their son Dave. Dave was in the U.S. Army, fighting in Vietnam, and was going to take his Rest and Recreation leave in Honolulu. After Tom Bushey found out about the trip, he placed a jar on the bar with a sign asking everyone to help Earl and June get to Hawaii and back. Tom also placed $100 in the jar to start off the donations.

🍺 🍺 🍺

While in Honolulu, Hawaii, Earl bought a carved wooden statue of a native with a huge penis, that hung down to his ankles. There was also a removeable shield covering the penis. When a female that he didn't know sat at the bar, Earl would place the statue in front of her and say, "My wife thinks they're all the same size." He would then remove the shield so they could see the huge penis. Rick Kellams said Earl pulled out the statue and told this joke every time he brought a new date to see Earl at the bar.

Earl's Wooden Native Statue

If you came into the bar and introduced Earl to your wife or girlfriend, Earl often told that wife or girlfriend, "You could have gotten a bartender if you had waited."

🍺 🍺 🍺

The distilled alcoholic beverage Whisky or Whiskey is spelled differently depending upon where the liquor is produced. In the United States and Ireland, it is spelled without the *e*, as in Whisky. While in Canada and Scotland the term Whiskey with an *e* is used. Earl at his bars would ask someone to spell Whisky. This would lead to Earl pulling out various bottles with the two different names, and an explanation as to why the names are different.

🍺 🍺 🍺

Earl performed quite a few magic tricks in his bars. He would show you a half dollar coin, and let you hold and touch it to make sure it was real. He would then miraculously punch the coin into a clear, glass liquor bottle, even though the coin was much larger than the mouth of the bottle.

🍺 🍺 🍺

In another magic trick, Earl would flick ashes from his cigarette onto the bar top, then dramatically hit the ashes with his fist, thereby driving the ashes through the bar and into the palm of his other hand, which was under the bar.

🍺 🍺 🍺

There was also a magic trick Earl called invisible fire. Earl would pull a piece of foil off of his cigarette pack, roll it up in a little ball on the bar, and bet someone a drink that they couldn't hold it in their hand for one minute. What they didn't know is that Earl had rolled the foil in a liquid that created intense heat. Everyone who took the bet dropped the foil almost as soon as it touched their hand, except Earl's good friend Judge Fred Spencer. Fred held the foil in the palm of his hand until it burnt and blistered his skin.

Earl, if asked to make a dry martini, put on quite a show. He would take out a stainless-steel cocktail shaker, dramatically add ice and pour both gin and vermouth into the shaker, place the lid and strainer on top of the shaker, and shake the container vigorously. Next, he would add an olive to a martini glass and turn the shaker over to fill the glass. To everyone's surprise nothing came out of the shaker, and the customer was handed a martini glass holding only an olive.

People liked and respected Earl, so his customers were typically on good behavior at his bars and fights were rare. If a fight did break out Earl knew, through experience, how to stop it. His goal though was to stop trouble and fights before they started. He always kept his eyes open, looking for any hints of an argument or disagreement, and he would calmly defuse these situations. To this end he did not allow anyone in his bars to use foul language, discuss politics or religion, and card playing was strictly prohibited unless of course it was Earl playing high stakes gin rummy.

Earl's wife June remembers being in the bar and hearing Earl say, "My nose is twitching." Typically within a few minutes, Earl would be at one of the tables, or the bar seats, to break up a heated discussion or argument.

When Earl was young and a fight started, he would jump over the bar and stop the fight. As he got older, he walked over and talked to the fighters.

Earl's wife June once asked Earl, "What happened to you Earl? You used to jump over the bar and throw them out the door, now you walk around and ask them to leave."

Leo Campbell was drinking at the Olympia Lounge when two people, on barstools beside him, started fighting. The fight quickly spiraled out of control and Leo was knocked off of his bar stool, and onto the floor. Earl jumping over the bar, broke up the fight and escorted the two fighters outside. As Leo slowly got up from the floor, he started complaining that his leg hurt. He continued drinking all that evening although he talked constantly about how much his leg hurt. The next day Leo went to the emergency room and found out he had a broken leg.

The Trade Winds Bar (Earl's first bartending job was at the Trade Winds)

The Trade Winds bar on old skid row, in Anderson, Indiana, was where Earl first started bartending in the 1940s. Beer, Earl said, was twenty-five cents a bottle and whiskey thirty-five cents a glass. One of Earl's customers at the Trade Winds borrowed five dollars and didn't pay Earl back. Earl kept asking for the money, but after a month realized that he would most likely never get his money back. Earl, hence, told the guy that he was going to beat his butt the next time he saw him. The guy must have thought getting his butt beat was worth five dollars, as he told Earl that was ok because after he got his butt beat, they would be even. Earl told him to forget it.

Duane Cox and Dave Alger were scared one night while bartending, without Earl, at the Tunnel Bar. An unknown man walked in the front door, down the length of the bar, and then behind the bar before reaching under his coat and pulling out a handgun. Duane and Dave froze, thinking they were going to be shot and robbed. The man then placed the gun on the bar and said, "Earl always makes me check my gun."

🍺 🍺 🍺

Another time while Duane was bartending at the Tunnel Bar, he noticed a customer with brass knuckles on his hand. The customer was drinking beer, singing along with the juke box, and tapping the brass knuckles on top of the bar. You never knew who you would see, or what type of people you would meet at Earl's bars. Everyone was welcome as long as they didn't start trouble.

🍺 🍺 🍺

The Tunnel Bar (Earl leased this bar for a short time)

🍺 🍺 🍺

Leonard Sharp came into the Tunnel Bar when Dean Alger was bartending and asked for a White Russian cocktail. As a new bartender, Dean had no idea how to mix this drink until Leonard explained it was vodka, Kahlúa, and cream served on the rocks. Leonard drank quite a few of these cocktails that evening and ended up stumbling out of the bar feeling no pain. Leonard the next day told Dean he had one hell of a hangover and joked that he must have been served some bad milk.

🍺 🍺 🍺

After closing the bar, Earl would sometimes stay behind and play gin, often until early in the morning. The gambling pot at times would reach $1,000 per hand. On one occasion the bar was raided by the Anderson Police Department vice squad and Earl was arrested for running a gaming house, while Earl Lawson the other card player was arrested for gambling. Vice squad Sergeants Charles Weatherly and Louis Lacey conducted the raid and arrested both Earls. The officers confiscated about $2,000 dollars during the raid. The charge against Earl Alger was eventually dismissed. He did however plead guilty to a violation of the 1935 Beverage Act and was fined twenty-one dollars. Opel Gilliam, a local politician, and Alger family friend made sure the confiscated $2,000 was returned to the card players.

🍺 🍺 🍺

Earl often gambled at the bar with Bill Collins, manager of the Anderson, Indiana Elk Lodge. On one occasion Earl was ahead all night, and Bill ended up losing his cash and writing a check to cover his remaining debt. They finished gambling early in the morning, and Earl went home and had breakfast. Before Earl got into bed, Bill knocked on Earl's door and asked to borrow $500. The rumor is that Bill needed the money to replenish the cash register, so he could open up the Elk bar that morning. Earl of course loaned Bill the $500.

🍺 🍺 🍺

Dave Imel, one of Earl's friends and a General Manager at Guide Corporation, spent a lot of time in the Olympia Lounge drinking, talking to Earl, and watching Earl play gin rummy. Although Dave was not a good gin player, and maybe not even an average player, he decided to try gambling at gin rummy. After finding a guy to play against, Dave asked for Earl's help and together they formulated a plan. It was agreed that Earl would stand by Dave during the game, and Dave would pick up a card from the discard pile whenever Earl tapped Dave's foot. Dave ended up winning the game and the cash. He also told Earl the foot tapping ruined his brand new Florsheim dress shoes.

🍺 🍺 🍺

A guy with the nickname Sarge regularly showed up at the Olympia Lounge to play cards with Earl. Sarge never beat Earl at gin rummy, and he likely gambled with Earl solely because it was entertaining, and he enjoyed Earl's company. Once while playing cards at the bar with Sarge, Earl got busy and stopped the game to make drinks for customers. Sarge finished this game playing Earl's wife June, who beat him out of $20. Sarge became the butt of many bar room jokes, with jokesters teasing him that he couldn't beat Earl or his wife.

🍺 🍺 🍺

Earl's life changed tremendously upon his retirement after fifty years of tending bar. When he talked about his life as a bartender, and how often his wife June was upset at his drinking, gambling, and long workdays Earl would say, "I got home every morning from work and the door was locked. I had donuts for the kids, they had already gone to school."

🍺 🍺 🍺

At other times Earl would say, "After retiring from bartending, I am getting up at the same time I got home for fifty years."

🍺 🍺 🍺

CHAPTER 2
EARL AND HIS FRIENDS

Earl had many loyal friends that absolutely loved him, and he loved them just as much. Some of these friends were Doug Davis, Norm Held, Joe Peoples, Bill Pitts, Jim Melson, Bill Rodgers, Fred Spencer, and Don Woods. After they both retired, Norm Held and Earl would have a few drinks most weeks at one of the local bars. Norm also organized birthday parties for Earl at these bars. As Earl aged into his eighties and nineties there were many hospital and rehab stays, and Doug Davis, Norm Held, Joe Peoples, and Fred Spencer were always there to visit Earl. Doug Davis, whenever Earl was in the hospital or rehab would visit every night, showing up about 8 or 9 P.M. and staying until midnight or later. Earl, worried about his wife June getting tired from staying at the hospital or rehab, would send her home by saying something like, "Doug will be here soon June, why don't you go home and get some rest." Bill Pitts honored his friend Earl using his outdoor sign and billboard at the Lemon Drop restaurant. If you drove past the Lemon Drop on Earl's birthday or Earl and June's wedding anniversary, Bill would make sure it was announced on the billboard. When Earl died, Bill posted on the billboard, "Earl Alger, Gone but Never Forgotten, 1923 – 2018.

🍺 🍺 🍺

Earl and Melvin "Bud" Biddle grew up together and remained friends all of their lives. Bud was awarded the Medal of Honor, our country's highest military decoration, during World War II for his acts of valor at the Battle of the

Bulge. Bud told multiple members of the Alger family, including Earl and June, that President Truman whispered in his ear as he presented Bud with the Medal of Honor that he would rather have the medal than be the president.

🍺 🍺 🍺

Earl Kisses Bud Biddle While Bud's Wife Leona Watches (Bud is wearing his Congressional Medal of Honor)

🍺 🍺 🍺

Dave Alger first met Bud Biddle at the Madison County courthouse, where Bud was being honored for his heroic actions during World War II. It was a crowded event attended by family and friends, state and local politicians, active military personnel and veterans, and people just wanting to meet and shake hands with a war hero awarded the Medal of Honor. Dave when he got the opportunity introduced himself as Earl's son. Bud smiled, moved Dave away from the crowd, and started talking about his good friend Earl Alger. He especially wanted to know how Earl was doing as he had not seen Earl in a while. Bud was quite a man and one of Earl's oldest friends.

🍺 🍺 🍺

Basketball Coach Norm Held was one of Earl's best friends. He coached the Anderson High School Indians for eighteen years, took his teams to four state finals, and had a record of 343 wins to 114 losses. More important though he was a good man. Norm frequently invited Earl to watch his team play ball. Earl was a big fan of the Indians basketball team but always told Norm he had to work during Friday game nights. Norm got tired of Earl's excuses and sent two police officers to Earl's bar, where they arrested him and placed him in handcuffs. The officers then drove Earl to the gym and at the team bench announced, "Coach, here's your prisoner." Norm then gave Earl a red and green Anderson Indians rally towel and sat him on the first row behind the bench.

🍺 🍺 🍺

When Earl was in his eighties, Norm Held arranged a birthday party for Earl at the R Bar in Anderson, Indiana. It was a small gathering of Earl's close friends, and two of Earl's sons Dave and Dean. Norm bought a birthday cake, and everyone had a piece of cake and a few drinks in celebration of Earl's birthday. Dean drove the newly restored MGA to the event so everyone could see it. As the group was talking about the car Earl commented, "Dean… why would you put all of that money into a $250 car?" Earl said this because he had paid $250 for the MGA in 1964. Dean replied that this was his first car, and therefore it was priceless to him. When Norm went outside to see the car, he turned to Dean and said, "I'll give you $300 cash right now for the MG. You'll make fifty dollars."

Norm Held at Earl's Cigar and Coffee Shop

Earl often repeated his jokes, but no matter how many times he told a joke people would laugh. If Earl repeated a joke around Norm Held, Norm would say, "I have heard that one, it's joke number thirty-seven." The numbers of course would change as Norm was just throwing out random numbers.

Tom Taylor, Earl's nephew, said that "Earl could say the same thing others said but you would laugh at how witty and funny Earl made it sound. That's a gift."

Bill Wallace when told about this book, and asked to provide any stories that he may know of for the book, responded, "Hope he didn't put everything he knew about me in there."

Ron Bryson and his wife Lorrie, long-time Alger family friends, often visited Earl at his bars. Ron said Earl would joke with Lorrie that he would do her once…but after that he would have to charge her.

Whenever Bob Mullins saw Earl, no matter where it was at, Bob would shout out, "Earl, you should be hung." "I am. I am," Earl would respond.

Another friend of Earl's always called him, "goddamn Earl."

Earl loved to make people smile and laugh, as Andrew Briggs can tell you. Andy was Dean Alger's college roommate and has been a good friend of the Alger family for over forty years. He spent a lot of time at Earl and June's home, especially during holidays and on special occasions. After Andy married his wife Rhonda, and for the next seventeen years whenever Earl would see or talk to Andy, the first thing Earl would say to Andy was, "Are you still married?" To this day Andy still smiles and laughs if this is mentioned to him.

🍺 🍺 🍺

Andrew Briggs and Earl (left to right Andrew and Earl)

🍺 🍺 🍺

Martha Baker Green would visit Earl at his coffee and cigar shop, in downtown Anderson, Indiana. One time near Christmas, Earl began telling Martha and some other people what the holidays meant to him during the Great Depression. Earl said he was from a poor family and Santa Claus didn't come to his house. There were no presents and no toys, but his mother would cut a hole in his pants pocket, so he had something to play with. After the laughter died down, Earl told them that by New Year's Day his mom would sew it (his pocket) back up. She didn't want him getting too spoiled.

Earl as a Child Playing with Something in His Pocket

One of Earl's customers and friends was a big, tough man and full-blooded Native American. Earl often called his friend Chief, without meaning it in a derogatory manner. After Earl died, the man told his grandson, Tim Carpenter, that "Earl Alger was the only man I ever let call me Chief."

Earl's friends were loyal. One couple would always stop in the bar on Earl's birthday, as the wife's birthday was on the same day, and she wanted to give Earl a kiss on their birthdays.

After the Olympia Lounge closed one night, a group of customers including Jim Melson went out for breakfast. Earl and his son Dave came in after the group had finished eating, and Earl jokingly told Jim Melson, "It's too bad you have already eaten, I was going to buy you breakfast." Jim's response was that he could eat two breakfasts. He then sat down with Earl and Dave and ordered the same meal he had just finished.

Earl drank vodka with a splash of Fresca, a grapefruit-flavored soft drink. When one of Earl's bartenders was making him a drink he would tell them, "don't bruise it," meaning add only a splash of Fresca to the drink.

Earl always stirred his own drink with his index finger. People would laugh at this and Earl would tell them, "I save $100 a year by not using swizzle sticks and stirring drinks with my index finger. Every three months my fingernail falls off, but it always grows back."

Jim Melson, according to Mark Szalaiy, would mix a special cocktail during their family gatherings. After pouring the liquor and other ingredients into cocktail glasses, Jim would finish off each drink by mixing it with his index finger. The family loved this drink, especially the way Jim stirred it, and started calling the drink a Melson. Jim passed away in 2000, the Melson cocktail however lives on as the Szalaiy family still makes them, laughing and stirring each drink just like Jim did. It appears Jim borrowed Earl's cocktail stirring method as well as the joke, and it is still getting laughs to this day.

🍺 🍺 🍺

Earl with Jim Melson and Bill Sebree (left to right Jim, Bill, and Earl)

🍺 🍺 🍺

While at the Olympia Lounge George Griswold borrowed $100 from Earl. This was a lot of money to Earl and his family, but Earl gladly loaned George the money since they were friends. After getting Earl's $100, George went to the restroom and came back to his barstool and got Earl's name wrong. He called him Carl, not Earl. This story turned into one of the running jokes that Earl told at the bar.

🍺 🍺 🍺

Virldeen Redmon, a longtime customer and friend of Earl's, was arrested at least 400 times, and over 230 times for alcohol related charges. He lost his driver's license for life and went to prison for many years on drunk driving charges. At one of Virldeen's many bail hearings in Anderson, Indiana, the judge Donald Phillippe was one of Earl's friends, and the prosecuting attorney was Earl's son Dave. After the bail was set, Virldeen pulled out a check to pay for his bail. Judge Phillippe reprimanded Virldeen telling him "Virldeen, you know the court will not take a check, as there may not be enough funds in your account to cover the check." Virldeen responded, "Of course the check is good. The prosecutor's father Earl Alger gave it to me."

🍺 🍺 🍺

Ward Davis was a horse trainer and handicapper out of Ohio. He gave Earl a tip that he said couldn't lose. Earl took Ward's advice and bet the horse to win. The horse was fast and winning the race…until the jockey fell off.

🍺 🍺 🍺

Earl, it seemed, knew people everywhere. Another time Earl and June walked into a Jai-Alai fronton in Florida, and someone across the court yelled, "hello Earl."

One of Earl's friends decided to quit taking diet pills that he called "Ole Yellow," and bought for a dollar per box. He was at his lake home in northern Indiana when he made this decision and threw the pills in the lake, and watched the ducks eat them. Earl's friend said he didn't get any sleep that night as the ducks quacked and quacked and swam in circles all night.

Earl and June's neighbor, Jerry Fuller, was a heavy drinker. He made good money working at Delco Remy but drank his money away. Jerry was paid on Friday and broke by Monday. Hence, Jerry borrowed twenty dollars from Earl every Monday morning, and always paid him back on Friday after work, before he started drinking. This went on for quite a few months prior to Earl telling Jerry, "Put twenty dollars in my mailbox on Friday, and it will be there for you on Monday when you need the money." Unbelievably this system worked.

When Dave Alger was sworn in as an attorney the oath to new attorneys was administered by the Indiana Supreme Court, and Earl's friend Donald Hunter was an Indiana Supreme Court Judge. Justice Donald Hunter was a regular at

Earl's bars, stopping in most evenings after work to see Earl and have a drink. During the luncheon part of the attorney swearing-in ceremony, Justice Hunter left the front dignitary table and walked over to Earl, June, and Dave. As he took a seat he said, "I want to eat lunch with my bartender, not the stuffy people." Justice Hunter after lunch introduced Earl, June, and Dave to the Lieutenant Governor who was also in attendance.

Newspaper Advertisement for Earl's Birthday

Glenn Keeney was a well-known martial artist and tenth Dan in Goju-Ryu karate. Multiple times Glenn was honored as one of the top fighters and instructors in the world. He was also a friend of Earl's and a regular customer at his bars.

When Glenn's name came up, Earl would tell a story about Glenn being in New York city, pulling his luggage down the street as he headed to his hotel, and two young hoodlums trying to rob him at knife point. Earl would say they picked the wrong man that day, and can you imagine how surprised they were when Glenn defended himself.

🍺 🍺 🍺

After closing the Olympia Cocktail Lounge for the night, Earl and June decided to go to breakfast at the Pony Express Restaurant. The Pony Express, owned by Earl's friend Tim Brandon, was a front for an illegal gambling operation in the restaurant's backroom. The gaming room had poker and dice tables, beer and liquor was also served. Earl, as soon as he finished eating, told June that he was going to the gambling room to collect a debt. As the gaming room door started to open because they knew Earl, undercover police officers stormed the door to get inside. The officers during their run for the door ended up shoving Earl inside the gambling room, and Earl was arrested, charged, and jailed for visiting a gambling establishment. Before the trial started though, the charge against Earl was dropped as Sheriff Deputy Modie Beeman, another friend of Earl's, testified that Earl was pushed into the gaming house.

🍺 🍺 🍺

Earl and June were at a wedding reception when Earl recognized a customer and friend at another table. Later that evening, Earl walked past the table and stopped by to say hello. In jest, Earl asked the guy if he still liked boys. People around the table thought it was funny and laughed. The guy, however, was mad at Earl.

🍺 🍺 🍺

Don Woods often called Earl at home. If Earl's wife June answered the phone, Don would start breathing heavy like there was a creepy pervert on the phone. June, unfazed by Don would laugh and just say "Don Woods" and put Earl on the phone.

🍺 🍺 🍺

Although Don Woods was not a medical doctor, he would often introduce himself as such and make restaurant and hotel reservations under the name Dr. Woods. Don would tell a story about being on vacation in Fort Lauderdale, Florida when hotel management called him, instead of an ambulance, after a guest injured their arm at the hotel swimming pool. Don went to the swimming pool, and acting like he knew what he was doing, started moving the fellow's arm around. In between screams the guy yelled, "Are you sure you're a doctor?"

🍺 🍺 🍺

Don Woods when he had breakfast at a restaurant would order two eggs, one sunny-side up and one down, and a glass of chocolate buttermilk. Most waitpersons would laugh at the order and tell Don they didn't have chocolate buttermilk. One resourceful young man however, poured Don a glass of buttermilk and walked over to a soda fountain pump where he put two squirts of chocolate syrup in the buttermilk.

🍺 🍺 🍺

It was not uncommon for one of Earl's friends, after an evening of drinking with Earl, to leave the bar to go home and quickly return to tell Earl that they had locked their keys in the car. Earl always asked if they had a spare set of keys and the normal response was that they did have a spare set of keys, but the keys were locked in the trunk of the car.

🍺 🍺 🍺

Duane Cox grew up with Dean Alger and was at the Alger family home all of the time. He was around so much in fact, that Earl and June, Dean's parents, treated Duane like one of their own children. If you attended an Alger family celebration, party, or holiday while Duane was alive, you likely saw Duane sitting on Earl and June couch, eating one of June's home cooked meals, and laughing. While in his forties Huntington's Disease handicapped Duane's mind and body, and he lost his independence and ability to financially support himself. It took a few years for Duane to get disability and health care from the government, but Earl and June bought a second house in Anderson and let Duane live there for free. Earl also regularly stopped in to see Duane and give him money, food, beer, cigarettes, and most important encouragement. Andrew Briggs and John "J.T." Thomas also helped Duane. Duane ended up in a nursing home and died at age 45. Towards the end of his life, Duane could not talk or get out of bed. He didn't usually recognize or acknowledge his visitors, but he always knew Earl, smiling brightly when he saw him and shaking his hand or hugging him.

🍺 🍺 🍺

At Earl's Cigar and Coffee Shop, Fred Spencer was a regular customer. He stopped in to see Earl, reminisce, and hear Earl's latest stories and jokes. Fred also brought his grandson Erick, who was four or five years old at the time, to the shop. Erick enjoyed seeing Earl and told his grandpa Fred, "If Earl ran for president, I would vote for him."

🍺 🍺 🍺

While June was in her fifties and in the hospital with cancer, friends of Earl's and June's, especially friends from Earl's bar, filled her hospital room with flowers.

🍺 🍺 🍺

Dr. Robert "Bob" Begley, a longtime friend of Earl's and the Alger family doctor, told Dean Alger a funny story about Earl and June. He said Earl was with June in the examination room when he told June she needed a chest x-ray. After he left the room, a nurse entered and asked June to put on a robe for the x-ray. Earl quickly said, "Do you want me stay in here while she disrobes." The nurse who did not know Earl and June said, "I guess so." And Earl responded with, "I'm just the taxicab driver and I didn't know if you wanted me in here or not." Dr. Begley said the nurse ran to his office and frantically declared that the taxicab driver was going to stay in the exam room while Mrs. Alger disrobes. Dr. Begley said he laughed and told her the taxicab driver was June's husband, and they had been married for over fifty years.

🍺 🍺 🍺

Earl was in the hospital for a knee replacement, and Dr. Begley stopped in to see Earl just before the surgery. The doctor that was going to conduct the surgery was noticeably young, so Earl said, "Are you sure he's old enough to be a doctor? I don't think I would even serve him in my bar." Dr. Begley laughed and Earl then said, "Has he ever performed a surgery like this before?" Dr. Begley without cracking a smile said, "No but he always wanted to."

🍺 🍺 🍺

Earl in his late eighties fell and broke his back and was in pain, twenty-four hours a day, the reminder of his life. He regularly took pain medication, prescribed by a doctor, although the pain was never completely eliminated. Numerous times Earl said he would like to try marijuana for pain relief. Dean Alger mentioned this to his friend Jim "Bird" Hiatt, and Bird quickly offered to make marijuana brownies for Earl. Bird also volunteered to taste them to make sure that they were not too strong. Keith Alfrey after listening to this conversation said he wasn't sure the brownies would get rid of Earl's pain, but he knew for sure that Earl wouldn't give a damn after eating them. Earl ultimately decided to pass on the marijuana brownies. He did, however, continue to take his prescribed pain medication.

🍺 🍺 🍺

As Earl was being wheeled, in a gurney, down a hospital hallway on the way to surgery, Doug Davis pulled a flask out of his pocket and offered Earl a shot of Tequila. Earl chuckled and said, "I don't think I should Doug."

🍺 🍺 🍺

Upon reaching midlife Earl put together a written pallbearer list, as a joke and also to honor his friends. Bill Pitts kept the list, supposedly for safekeeping, in his cash register at the Lemon Drop restaurant. As Earl started outliving the pallbearers (he lived longer than at least four pallbearers), alternates were added to the list. Earl's friends loved being on the list and it was so popular Earl would joke, "I should charge them." The list included Jim Anderson, Jeff Hardin, Norm Held, Bill Pitts, and Fred Spencer.

🍺 🍺 🍺

Earl Kissing Linda Davis While Jeff Harden Poses (photograph taken at Earl's Cigar and Coffee Shop)

🍺 🍺 🍺

Jeff Hardin really wanted to be one of Earl's pallbearers. After Earl told Jeff that he made the list Jeff said, "That's wonderful news and I can't wait." Earl never let Jeff forget that. Jeff, rightfully so, explained that Earl was greatly exaggerating the event.

🍺 🍺 🍺

The pallbearer list came up later after Earl had surgery. Earl's first words out of surgery were, "Get a hold of Bill Pitts (at the Lemon Drop) and tell him not to call the pallbearers."

🍺 🍺 🍺

Dean Alger, along with two of his friends, walked into the Columbia Club in downtown Indianapolis, Indiana. At the bar Dean noticed Jim Anderson, a friend of his dad's, and Dean led his group over to sit down next to Jim. After introductions were exchanged Dean and Jim started talking about Dean's dad, Earl, and his pallbearers, as Jim Anderson was on Earl's coveted pallbearer list. Dean's friends evidently heard some of this conversation, as they later told Dean they were sorry to hear that his dad had died. Dean laughed and explained that his dad was alive and well, but he had a pallbearer list that was kept in the cash register at the Lemon Drop, a popular restaurant in Anderson, Indiana. Dean went on to say, his dad had outlived so many of his pallbearers, that the list now includes alternates as well.

🍺 🍺 🍺

When the family did need the pallbearer list just after Earl died, Bill Pitts was called, and he said the list was gone. Someone had broken into the Lemon Drop restaurant and stole the cash register with the pallbearer list in it. Ultimately the family decided to have Earl's grandsons serve as pallbearers at his funeral, as the pallbearer list was missing, and the family was not exactly sure who was on the list.

🍺 🍺 🍺

Earl was somewhat of a father figure to Dick Dunn, and over the years Dick spent a lot of time in Earl's various bars. When Earl was in his nineties Dick worked at a local funeral home, and Earl would tell June that Dickey was going to take him on his last ride. While Dick did not normally drive the hearse, at the family's request, the funeral home allowed Dick to drive Earl to his gravesite. Dick said he talked to Earl and cried some, all the way to the cemetery.

🍺 🍺 🍺

Earl most nights at his bars got his friends together for celebratory shots of cherry brandy, and one of his highly anticipated and usually off-colored toasts. At Earl's funeral the children wanted to extend this tradition, so friends and family were invited to the gravesite for shots of cherry brandy and a farewell toast. This resulted in about fifty people gathered around Earl's coffin. As people finished their shots and started complaining to each other about the taste of cherry brandy, Earl's good friend Bill Pitts yelled out, "Let's have another one." Fortunately or unfortunately, depending on how much you like cherry brandy, more people showed up at the gravesite than expected and there wasn't enough cherry brandy for another toast.

🍺 🍺 🍺

Farewell Toast to Earl at His Gravesite (note the empty bottle of Cherry Brandy on Earl's coffin)

🍺 🍺 🍺

CHAPTER 3
EARL AND HIS FAMILY

Earl's father Frank Alger, like his son, loved a good joke. Frank once raffled off a turkey at work during the holidays. The guy that won the raffle found a live turkey in his locker the next day.

🍺 🍺 🍺

Ruby Simpson, June Alger's mother and Earl Alger's mother-in-law, was a passionate Republican. As a practical joke Frank Alger called Ruby's home, without telling her who was calling, and asked her, "Do you know that Jesus Christ was a Democrat?" Ruby responded with two words "Frank Alger" and Frank laughed like that was the funniest thing he had ever heard.

🍺 🍺 🍺

Frank Alger died at age fifty-six. Earl was twenty-nine years old at the time, and always said he thought his dad was an old man when he died.

🍺 🍺 🍺

At Frank Alger's funeral a young man attended that had walked to the service through heavy rain, and during a tornado warning. The man cried as he told Earl how kind Frank had been to him. The young man had just started working at Delco Remy, and Frank was teaching him how to be an electrician. Earl like his dad was a kind man.

🍺 🍺 🍺

In high school, Earl borrowed his father's car and took a group of friends out for a ride. Running low on gas these teenage boys decided, apparently without a lot of thought, that it would be a clever idea to steal some gasoline. As one might guess, they got caught while siphoning gas from a stranger's car. When the police showed up everyone ran except for Earl, who knew he needed to stay with his father's car. Earl was arrested and the incident was written up and reported in the local newspaper. Earl's wife June, who was his girlfriend at the time, said her mother read about the incident in the newspaper and asked, "Is this the young man you're dating?" Earl later redeemed himself with June's family in part by dropping off, on the front porch, an occasional case of soda when he was working for Pepsi Cola. June said this was quite a treat as the family could not afford soda.

🍺 🍺 🍺

After serving in the Army Air Corps during World War II, Earl was a short order cook and he loved cooking for the rest of his life. On weekends he cooked for his family. His specialty was fried chicken, which everyone loved. Earl's son Dean remembers his dad telling him, "If Colonel Sanders would've had my recipe…he would've been a general."

🍺 🍺 🍺

Earl would tell the following story about his lawn care skills, or maybe about fooling his wife June. "When I first got married, I mowed the lawn. My wife is very particular about her yard, and she didn't like the way I mowed it. Fifty years later she still wouldn't let me mow the lawn again."

🍺 🍺 🍺

Earl loved and was proud of his children. He would tell everyone that he and June had four kids in college at the same time, and they all graduated. Dave becoming an attorney, Dean a geologist, Doug a businessman, and Susie a nurse.

🍺 🍺 🍺

Earl with His Daughter Susie Erehart

🍺 🍺 🍺

When Dave Alger was in high school, he was often in trouble for fighting and drinking. Earl would tell people, "I don't know if Dave is going to jail, Vietnam, or college." Dave served in Vietnam with the Army 101st Airborne and graduated from college with both a bachelor's and doctoral degree. After becoming a criminal defense attorney, Dave often spent time in jails with his clients, so I guess Dave lived up to and even exceeded all of his dad's expectations.

🍺 🍺 🍺

Dave Alger, as a young attorney, was elected to the Anderson, Indiana school board. During his term on the school board, Dave helped develop a plan that would, in the next ten years, close Madison Heights High School and move Anderson High School (the Indians) into Madison Heights' newer school building. This plan was extremely controversial, and Earl's friends and customers let him know how much they disliked the idea. Earl as a result told Dave, "I've been a bartender in Anderson for over fifty years, and I may have to move out of town."

🍺 🍺 🍺

Dave Alger, an attorney in Anderson, Indiana, is well known for always being late, even to court. Earl would tell you, "If Dave is thirty minutes late, he's early."

🍺 🍺 🍺

Dean Alger often told people that he couldn't get a speeding ticket as a young man in Anderson. The police officer would pull him over, look at his driver's license, and ask "Are you Earl's son?" After Dean answered yes, the police officer would typically say something like, "Tell Earl hello and slow down."

🍺 🍺 🍺

Earl was amazed by and often told people that his son Doug and his wife Laura moved seventeen times in twenty-two years.

🍺 🍺 🍺

Earl loved to gamble, and he was good at it, especially billiards and gin rummy. Many family vacations to Florida were paid for using Earl's winnings from gambling. Earl won a lot and when someone asked Earl how he won so much, he would say, "I'm lucky and I cheat."

🍺 🍺 🍺

While he was a young man Earl asked his father about horse racing. His dad's response was, "Horses pull wagons and shit in the street, that's all you need to know about horse racing." It appears Earl listened to his dad's advice, as he rarely bet on horses and would joke that his brother-in-law Shannon Chambers was the best horse racing handicapper in town, and he lost more money than anyone else.

🍺 🍺 🍺

On a family vacation in Florida, Earl was at the dog track with two of his sons Dave and Dean. It was an uneventful day for the family with no big winners, until Earl placed a long shot bet on one of the dogs and the dog won. Earl, expecting a big payout, went to the betting window to cash his ticket, and was told he didn't win because the blankets on two dogs had been inadvertently switched. The dog Earl bet on, had actually run last.

🍺 🍺 🍺

Late in life Earl and June enjoyed going to the casino in Anderson, Indiana. At the casino they would play slot machines and socialize with friends, and Earl always drank a few cups of the free coffee. If one of Earl's friends asked about the casino he would tell them, "I went to the casino the other day and had a $100 cup of coffee." Sometimes he would tell them the coffee is now $200 because of inflation.

🍺 🍺 🍺

Dean Alger, and his wife Marianne, still laugh about playing cards with Earl and June. Marianne, with her cheerful personality, would often delay dealing the cards as she was talking instead of playing. Earl still thinking like a gambler, even though he was in his nineties and had quit gambling at card games, got tired of the talk and said, "shut up and deal."

🍺 🍺 🍺

Earl and June on many occasions took their kids to Cincinnati, Ohio for weekend vacations and to see the

Cincinnati Reds play baseball. On one of these mini vacations, while driving downtown and looking for an available hotel room, Earl said "I must know someone here that can help us." June with a laugh responded, "Earl you don't know anyone in Cincinnati." Immediately a man on a telephone pole yelled out, "Hey Earl" and waved at us.

Earl with His Sons (left to right Dave, Earl, Dean, and Doug)

During a Cincinnati Red's home game, Willie McCovey with the San Francisco Giants hit a homerun. Earl and his son Dave missed seeing McCovey hit the homerun, because they were at the concessions stand inside a stadium tunnel. They did nevertheless see the homerun ball as the ball went into the tunnel, knocked a beer out of Earl's hand, and bounced along the walkway. Earl outran another fan and grabbed the ball. This could only happen to a bartender.

🍺 🍺 🍺

Dave Alger in the MG

🍺 🍺 🍺

Sometime in 1964 Earl bought a 1959 MGA, a British two-seat convertible sportscar, for his wife June. The car was Glacier Blue, with a white top, wire wheels, and white leather seats. He said he got the car for $250 from Bill Ballard, although it is rumored that he won the car from Bill in a card game. Bill had bought the car for his wife, but she thought it was too hard to drive. Dave Alger remembers his dad saying,

"Bill Ballard's wife didn't like the MG, my wife didn't like it, but my sons sure do."

🍺 🍺 🍺

Dave Alger started driving the MG while he was in high school and continued to drive it until he left for Vietnam in 1969. When Dave's brother Dean got his driver's license, while Dave was in Vietnam, he took over the MGA. It didn't run at first, so Dean and his friends worked on the car to get it running and also learned some valuable mechanical skills while doing so. Younger brother Doug later drove the car and had it repainted a dark blue. Doug and Dean actually shared the MG while attending Ball State University and Indiana University. Eventually the engine blew, and the car sat for many years. The MGA was restored by Dean and Dave in 2007, and today it looks almost brand new. Earl was right, his sons do like the sports car he bought in 1964 for his wife.

🍺 🍺 🍺

Earl thought Marianne Bergamo, Dean's wife, could do anything and he told her quite often. He also told her, "If you had a penis, you would have been a millionaire."

🍺 🍺 🍺

Marianne Bergamo walked into Earl and June's house wearing perfume and Earl said, "It smells like a whore house in here." Marianne then asked Earl how he knew what a whore house smelled like, and Earl responded, "I used to play piano in one." Earl of course never played the piano.

🍺 🍺 🍺

Earl Admiring Marianne Bergamo's Figure

🍺 🍺 🍺

Matt Helping, while growing up, spent a lot of time with his grandparents Earl and June and was remarkably close to them. Earl in fact taught Matt how to drive a car. This may not sound unusual; however, Matt at the time was five years old. Matt would sit on Earl's lap and steer the car, while Earl worked the gas and brake pedals. They drove all over town that way and Matt rarely needed directions to most destinations. Matt got his first driving ticket at the age of five or six after a surprised policewomen pulled them over. She said she couldn't believe that Earl was letting Matt drive.

🍺 🍺 🍺

When Abby Rivers, Earl's granddaughter, introduced her fiancé Nick Rivers to her grandfather, Earl said, "Good to meet you, Dick." Abby then said, "No Pa his name is Nick." "Dick, that's what I said," Earl responded with a smile. Abby again tried to explain, but Earl interrupted her and said, "I am just going to call him lucky because he is lucky to have you."

🍺 🍺 🍺

Late in Earl's life, Earl was in his nineties, he lost most of his vision. Whenever Earl saw Abby Rivers, he would tell her she gets prettier every time he sees her. She would giggle to herself because she knew Earl couldn't see very well.

🍺 🍺 🍺

Connor "Max" Alger went to visit his grandparents, Earl and June, just after he turned twenty-one years old, the legal drinking age in Indiana. June, who has only had a few drinks in her life, decided she wanted to celebrate Connor's birthday by having a drink with him. After looking in freezer where Earl kept his vodka and not finding it, June asked Earl, "What happened to the Grey Goose Vodka in the freezer?" Earl thought for a few seconds and responded, "I don't know it must have evaporated." Although this is not gut busting funny, it is a classic Earl response and Connor enjoys remembering and talking about this.

🍺 🍺 🍺

Earl recognized that his granddaughter Lauren and her husband Zack Pratt had a special relationship and would say, "It would have been a shame if they hadn't met."

🍺 🍺 🍺

Earl would say, "Fifty years ago my brother-in-law was the prosecuting attorney, and I knew all the police. I could have shot six people and the police would have told me to go home, and they will call me if they need me."

🍺 🍺 🍺

Earl sometimes told a story about his brother-in-law Blondie Carey, and his wife Merle. Merle and Blondie were standing in a long line at the movie theater when Blondie loudly farted. As bystanders turned to look at him, Blondie looked at his wife and said, "well goddamn lady" and walked off. Merle refused to talk to Blondie for two weeks.

🍺 🍺 🍺

The first time Earl and June went to Las Vegas they stayed at Caesars Palace. Earl joked that Caesars Palace wanted a dollar for a beer, and there were mirrors over the bed, so June refused to take her clothes off for the three nights they stayed. Earl also talked about a homeless man with a sign that said, "Won't lie. Need a dollar for beer."

🍺 🍺 🍺

June Alger has always been very modest, even around her husband Earl. Because of this Earl would joke, "I have been married seventy-six years and never seen my wife naked." Martha Bormann, Earl and June's niece, said this was the funniest thing she ever heard Earl say.

🍺 🍺 🍺

Earl and June were on their way to Florida when they had what Earl called a "little spat." After they exchanged words, Earl saw a bar and went inside to have a beer, leaving June in the car. He said it was a horseshoe shaped bar with only two empty seats, which were next to each other. Earl took one of the empty seats, and after a while June came in and sat down next to Earl. She said something to Earl, and he responded in a loud voice, "fifty dollars." He then grabbed her hand, and they walked out together."

🍺 🍺 🍺

When Earl and June were in their sixties, June told Earl that she wanted to see Washington D.C. Earl's response was that they had already been to Washington D.C., and he mentioned some of the places that they had seen. June nonetheless was adamant that she had never been to D.C. Earl later showed June a picture of herself, with two of her young boys, sitting on the steps of the Lincoln Memorial. From that point forward, whenever June said she wanted to go somewhere new, Earl would tell her with a smile on his face that they had already been there.

🍺 🍺 🍺

"I told you I was sick." These last words were carved on B. P. Roberts' headstone. Ms. Roberts, a resident of Key West, Florida, was a hypochondriac and people teased her about her imaginary illnesses. Earl saw the headstone at the Key West Cemetery, while he and June were visiting Jerry Duncan and Betty Lawler at Jerry's home on the island. Earl enjoyed this comical headstone and would tell people about it.

If you asked Earl how he was, he would enthusiastically respond "fantastic." When Earl and June were on their Key West vacation, Earl was downtown one morning on a park bench, drinking coffee and reading the newspaper. A stranger walked up and asked Earl how he was, and Earl gave his typical "fantastic" response. The man must have misinterpreted the enthusiasm in Earl's voice, as he asked Earl if he wanted to have sex. Earl at the time was in his seventies and happily married to June for over fifty years.

Dean Alger took Earl home to Anderson, from a doctor's appointment in Indianapolis. Because of a urology procedure at the appointment, Earl felt like he needed to urinate even though his bladder was empty. As a result Earl asked the doctor's office for a bottle to urinate in. After Dean got the car on Interstate 69, headed towards Anderson, Earl started complaining that he had to pee. He then pulled his penis out of his pants and placed it in the urine bottle. Dean got a glancing view of this and quickly accelerated the car to get home as soon as possible, exceeding the speed limit in the process. Earl reaction was, "Dean, you better slow down so we don't have to explain this to a police officer."

🍺 🍺 🍺

Earl only had one colonoscopy during his ninety-six years, and he was awake and in pain during the procedure. As the doctor moved the scope through Earl's colon, Earl would yell out, and the doctor would tell his nurse to give Earl more sedation medication. This didn't relieve the pain though and Earl yelled out during the entire procedure. The next day Earl's arm swelled up to about twice its normal size. The doctor when he saw Earl's arm said the nurse inserting the IV had missed his vein, so Earl was unfortunately scoped without sedatives or pain medication.

🍺 🍺 🍺

Happy Birthday Sign for Earl at the Lemon Drop

🍺 🍺 🍺

Earl on his way to his ninety-fifth birthday party, fell on the walkway at the event center and wasn't feeling well at the party. Marianne Bergamo, wife of Earl's son Dean, walked up to Earl and asked, "Do you want me to take you home Earl?" Earl answered, "Sure…but what will we tell your husband."

🍺 🍺 🍺

As Earl got older, after he fell and broke his back, he needed a walker to get around. Earl would tell people that he had 80,000 miles on his walker. Judging by the way he quickly moved around with that walker, he might have been right.

🍺 🍺 🍺

Dan Spall was at Earl and June's seventieth wedding anniversary, and he noticed that Earl had a bottle of Cherry Brandy and plastic shot glasses in his walker's storage area. Dan said Earl moved around the room greeting people, and as he talked to each person, he would lift up the seat on his walker and offer them a Cherry Brandy. He was still a bartender even in his nineties.

🍺 🍺 🍺

For Earl and June's seventy-fifth wedding anniversary the family celebrated by having a big party. Earl was about ninety-four years old, and he invited women to the party by telling them, "There's a ten-dollar cover charge to attend…but it's free if you come topless."

🍺 🍺 🍺

Earl was a bartender and bar owner for over fifty years. He worked long hours, drank vodka, and smoked cigarettes. In fact, he smoked from age thirteen to ninety years old. It was not a healthy lifestyle, but Earl lived to be ninety-five years old. So when Earl was in his eighties and nineties, and someone asked him his secret to a long life, he would answer, "clean living."

🍺 🍺 🍺

Earl's wife June complained about her husband's smoking for many years. Earl said he got away with smoking by telling her, "I'm going to smoke this year and the next and then quit." She finally wised up he said, so he told her, "I'll quit when we get back from Michigan." She asked when are we going to Michigan, and he told her "We're not."

🍺 🍺 🍺

A minister from June's church stopped by to see Earl in the hospital. As they talked the minister asked, "Do you attend church regularly?" Earl without missing a beat said, "I am a regular church goer. I attend every Easter but missed the last two."

🍺 🍺 🍺

Earl in his seventies had droopy eyelids that restricted his vision. To improve his eyesight a local doctor performed a brow lift on Earl. The procedure was completed while Earl was awake and involved drilling two holes in his forehead and inserting titanium screws. Earl of course made a joke out of this, by telling people he had a screw loose in his head. He would then allow them to feel one of the screws in his forehead, which usually resulted in disbelief and laughter.

When Earl and June reached their nineties Earl would tell people, "If anyone would have told me that I was going to be sleeping with ninety-year-old woman, I would have slapped them."

Earl told his family that he disliked hospitals because people die in them. He also said he doesn't even like driving past a hospital or cemetery.

Late in life Earl was in the hospital over Christmas. His wife and many of his children, even a grandchild Connor Alger, were in the hospital room with him on Christmas Eve. Betty Lawler, June's sister, and Earl's sister-in-law, also came to the hospital with her daughter Jean Zaiser, Jean's husband Breck Zaiser, and their two children Jordon and Luke. Wonderful conversation followed, stories and jokes were told, and people laughed. Breck, a career U.S. Army sergeant in the Special Forces, gave Earl a baseball style hat from the Army 7th Special Forces Group. Earl appreciated the cap but never wore it because he said he didn't earn it. Breck was a true "man's man" Earl would say. At the end of the evening, Jean's family started singing Christmas carols and everyone joined in. Earl, even though he was in the hospital at the time, always told his family that this was one of his best Christmases.

During another hospital stay, this time for pneumonia, Earl's kidneys failed. Doctors had drained fluid from his lungs and were administering high doses of an antibiotic when the kidney failure took place. Earl needed emergency dialysis to save his life but didn't want the dialysis. Further, the doctors told the family that they didn't expect his kidneys to recover or for him to live very long, even with dialysis as elderly people do not handle dialysis well. The family, despite this bad news from the doctors, were not ready to lose Earl and they wanted him to give the dialysis a go. Dave Alger even told his father, "Try the dialysis for five treatments dad, and if you don't want to continue them, I'll put the pillow over your head myself." After this Earl did try the dialysis, his kidneys recovered, and he lived another eight years or so. Upon being told that his kidneys had recovered, and he no longer needed dialysis, Earl thanked the doctor. The doctor though pointed his finger up in the air, and said, "I didn't do anything, thank him."

Melda Goodman was Dave Alger's mother-in-law, and also managed his law office. She was a wonderful lady and friends with the entire Alger family. At Melda's funeral her children read notes that Melda had written for her children, on how to live life. Dean Alger after the funeral told Melda's daughter and Dave's ex-wife, Leann Jones, that the notes her mother left on living life were absolutely beautiful, while his dad Earl left his children dirty jokes written on scraps of paper.

🍺 🍺 🍺

Marianne Bergamo was helping her mother-in-law, June Alger, plan her funeral. When Marianne asked June if there was any special outfit she wanted buried in, Earl spoke up, "Have you ever thought about going topless June?"

🍺 🍺 🍺

When Earl was in his nineties, and with his son Dean at a funeral service, he joked "Everyone is looking at me. They think I'm next."

🍺 🍺 🍺

Earl would say, "I want to die at 2713 Apache Drive." This was Earl and June's home address, where they raised their children and lived for over sixty-five years.

🍺 🍺 🍺

Dean Alger was with his father Earl, when Earl found out from his doctor that he had terminal cancer. On the ride home from the doctor's office, Earl told Dean, "I'm not afraid to die, but I don't want it to happen today or tomorrow."

🍺 🍺 🍺

After Earl died Dean Alger found a photograph in a family keepsake box of two camels humping. The photograph was yellow and faded, and clearly very old. When Dean asked his mother why this photograph was being saved, Dean was told his grandfather, Frank Alger, had carried the photo in his wallet for many years, and Dean's father, Earl, decided to keep the same photo in his wallet after Frank's death. Although there is likely some sort of story or joke associated with this photo, no one alive today has any idea what story or joke that might be. Thanks to Dean Alger all of Earl's sons and grandsons have copies of this photograph, and most of them keep the photograph in their wallet.

🍺 🍺 🍺

Earl was buried at Anderson Memorial Park in Anderson, Indiana. For over four and one-half years the cemetery has been unable to get grass to fully grow on Earl's grave. The cemetery has tried multiple applications of seeds and fertilizer, but the resulting grass is only spotty at best. Dave Alger has joked, "Earl was a drinker and bartender, so it must be all of the alcohol seeping out of his body that is killing the grass."

🍺 🍺 🍺

CHAPTER 4
EARL'S JOKES

Bartending and Drinking

"I was going to be a brain surgeon, but my family wanted me to learn a trade…so I became a bartender."

"I quit General Motors in the 1940s while making thirty-five dollars a week for a forty-hour work week and went to work bartending making seventy-five dollars a week and working one hundred hours each week."

"I started bartending for one dollar per hour, free drinks, and a little strange stuff. Best job I ever had."

"Do you know the difference between a bartender and everyone else? About two inches." Earl would hold his thumb and forefinger apart two inches when he told this joke. Earl told his son Dean, as they discussed this joke, "I don't tell them which way."

"I'm just a dumb bartender with a big peter."

🍺 🍺 🍺

"I drink vodka…it makes your peter grow."

🍺 🍺 🍺

"I had my first drink at the bar tonight with the glass in my right hand, standing on my left foot, and facing southwest."

🍺 🍺 🍺

"I drink enough to keep a small bar going."

🍺 🍺 🍺

"If no one shows up at the bar…we will still do good business."

🍺 🍺 🍺

"It's mine (the glass), I can wash it as fast as I want to."

🍺 🍺 🍺

Earl would joke about his employees, "If they didn't drink…I couldn't use them."

🍺 🍺 🍺

"Never hire a bartender that sings 'put in a nickel, take out a dime, and soon this place is all mine.'"

"There are two new songs on the juke box: 'Don't Let Your Meatloaf' and 'It was South of the Border and She Still Came Across.'"

"The last tip I got ran fifth."

"One hundred customers that never had $100 on the same day, wanted to buy a bar and have me run it."

"You can tell if a customer is drunk, by putting down change for ten dollars and asking them if it was five-dollar bill or ten-dollar bill. If they quickly say it was a ten-dollar bill, they are drunk, because it was a twenty-dollar bill."

Earl closed the bar many nights by exclaiming, "It's time to go home, June just called, and she has nothing on but the television."

🍺 🍺 🍺

"For fifty years I told them if anyone fought, it had to be me, and I can't whip my wife."

🍺 🍺 🍺

"Fifty years ago everyone had guns but me."

🍺 🍺 🍺

"I told the bouncer I'll get the little one…he might have a knife."

🍺 🍺 🍺

"If you leave, you're going to miss the dancing girls. There are thirteen dancing girls and twelve costumes."

🍺 🍺 🍺

"Free drinks tomorrow."

🍺 🍺 🍺

"There's no need to drink on New Year's Eve…it's amateur's night."

🍺 🍺 🍺

"I am going to drink this year and next year…and then I'm quitting."

🍺 🍺 🍺

"Indiana University wants my liver."

🍺 🍺 🍺

"Beer…you never own it…you just rent it."

🍺 🍺 🍺

"Beer…it all comes out of the same horse."

🍺 🍺 🍺

"A customer asked me to call him a cab, and I said to him 'you're a cab.'"

🍺 🍺 🍺

"Men have made three mistakes with women. They've allowed them to vote, drive, and go to taverns."

🍺 🍺 🍺

"I walked into the bar's bathroom to pee. As I was peeing a man ran to the urinal next to me, pulled out a ten inch long and two inch around penis and said, 'I just made it.' I looked down at it and exclaimed, 'Can you make me one just like it?'"

🍺 🍺 🍺

"Think of a number between one and ten." Earl would ask female customers this question and no matter how they answered he would say, "You lose …take your clothes off."

🍺 🍺 🍺

"I give away peter and bubble gum."

🍺 🍺 🍺

"When I told a customer that I had been in Hawaii, he asked me if I flew. I told him, 'No…I drove.'"

🍺 🍺 🍺

With wet hands, Earl would shake a customer's hand and say, "The darndest thing just happened to me. I was in the restroom and pissed all over myself." Sometimes Earl would next say, "You think I'm kidding, don't you?"

🍺 🍺 🍺

"I met a couple that were good people and became good customers and friends. They got married and one year later had kids. The kids turned twenty-one and the couple brought them into the bar to meet me. Later the kids get married, have kids, the kids turn twenty-one and they bring them into the bar to meet me. I have been here too long."

🍺 🍺 🍺

"For my fifty years in the bar room, I just wanted to fool them all the time anyway."

🍺 🍺 🍺

"For fifty years I worked fifteen hours a day, never late, missed one or two days of work, drank two quarts of booze every day, and smoked two or three packs of cigarettes a day."

🍺 🍺 🍺

Health

"At the hospital I had eight doctors…and one of them could speak English."

🍺 🍺 🍺

"I only have two bad habits…smoking and lying."

🍺 🍺 🍺

"Cancer cures smoking."

🍺 🍺 🍺

"Don't drink water. Fish screw in it."

🍺 🍺 🍺

Money

"Money is not important…until you run out."

🍺 🍺 🍺

I've got enough money to last me the rest of my life…if I die before midnight."

🍺 🍺 🍺

"All of my money is invested in pussy, booze, and hillbilly music…although not exactly in that order."

🍺 🍺 🍺

"I don't trust banks. I carry all of my money in my pocket."

🍺 🍺 🍺

"If you owe the bank $1,000, they own you. If you owe the bank $50,000, you own them."

🍺 🍺 🍺

"I'm going to have to work a half day on the day I die."

🍺 🍺 🍺

"If you want money late in life, don't buy anything that eats."

Old Age

"For fifty years I worked fifteen or sixteen hours a day as a bartender. I'm going to be ninety-five years old, but I'm really 105 with all the overtime I've worked."

"I am at an age where I get my age and I.Q. mixed up."

"At my age…I don't buy green bananas."

"If I was a horse… they would shoot me."

"Years ago, when I was a kid, I was tall and good-looking. Now I'm ninety-five years old and fat."

"I have knee trouble. The left knee is ok, and the right knee is ok, but I have trouble with the weinee."

🍺 🍺 🍺

"When I started bartending beer cost twenty-five cents, and whiskey thirty-five cents."

🍺 🍺 🍺

"Die tomorrow no big deal. Nursing home bad."

🍺 🍺 🍺

"I am ninety-five years old and have seen some amazing things during my life. Jet planes now fly people all over the world and men walked on the moon, but there is nothing like indoor plumbing."

🍺 🍺 🍺

Wife and Marriage

"I've been married for seventy-six years. That's a world record for a bartender."

"I didn't find out about the difference between boys and girls until I got married and never stepped out on my wife. I'm sort of like a virgin."

"I've been married seventy-six years and my wife thinks they're all the same size. They're all the size of roasting ears.

"I give my wife a breast exam for cancer every morning. Not only have I saved her life, it's also hard to be mad at the person that just gave you a breast exam."

"My wife ran away with my best friend. I sure miss him."

"If the wife thinks you're not coming home. Knock on the front door and run around back."

🍺 🍺 🍺

"All of my kids look like their father. We just don't know who their father is."

🍺 🍺 🍺

"I have the oldest dog in the world. I've been married to her for seventy-six years."

🍺 🍺 🍺

"My wife thinks I started World War II."

🍺 🍺 🍺

When a friend or customer asked Earl how his wife June was Earl would say, "June who?"

🍺 🍺 🍺

Earl carried in his wallet a fake newspaper advertisement that he would show to people. The ad read, "Set of encyclopedias for sale. Bought new and never used. Wife knows everything."

🍺 🍺 🍺

"I am a go getter. I take my wife to work and go get her when she is done."

🍺 🍺 🍺

If introduced to a married couple from Kentucky, Tennessee, or one of the other southern states Earl would say, "Are you still brother and sister?"

🍺 🍺 🍺

Sports

"In high school I was too small for most sports, but I was good at two of them: broad jumping and javelin catching. As a javelin catcher, you would throw the javelin and then run and catch it."

"I did a lot of fighting, in Golden Gloves boxing matches, until I had trouble with my hands. The referee kept stepping on them."

"Have you heard the joke about the one-armed fisherman? He caught a fish this big." Earl would hold only one arm high in the air as he said this last sentence.

Sex

"Do you know what Adam's first words to Eve were? You better stand back because we don't know how big this thing is going to get." Earl always said this was the first joke ever told.

"I ate a dozen oysters on the half shell…only ten worked."

Earl would sometimes marry couples in the bar using the *Old Mr. Boston Official Bartender's Guide*. After having his customers gather around the couple, Earl would ask the couple to place their hands on top of book and he would then say a few risqué words to publicly proclaim that they were married. Lastly, he would tell everyone the marriage is only good for the weekend.

While giving a free drink to a female customer Earl might say, "The first time is free…the second time I've got to charge you."

When talking about sex with his female customers, Earl might joke, "You have to get something straight between you" or "Let's get something straight between us."

"I'm not long to get hard with." This was one of Earl's favorite lines.

"My waitress had two chances to get pregnant. She blew them both."

"My waitress is sitting on a million dollars."

"When I was a teenager, a nice fairy gave me a choice between a big peter or a good memory. I don't remember which one I chose."

"Do you know the difference between free sex and sex you have to pay for? You can't afford free sex."

"Sex is nice in the morning, sex is nice when going to bed, but sometimes don't you think a matinee is nice."

"Why walk when you can ride for a piece."

"I only wiggle lying down." Andy Alger, Earl's grandson, loved this one-liner.

"The first tee shirt ever made had an inscription on the front saying, 'I am a Virgin' and on the back 'This is an Old Shirt.'"

An old urban legend was still circulating, when Earl was in his sixties and seventies, that the military during World War II added saltpeter to soldier's food to control their sexual urges. With that in mind Earl would tell people, "The army gave me saltpeter while I was a soldier… and it just started working."

"Indiana has some interesting cities. North Vernon is not north, South Bend is not south, and French Lick is not what it sounds like."

🍺 🍺 🍺

"Don't chase single girls, they've got jealous boyfriends. Get a married one."

🍺 🍺 🍺

Questions

"Easy job…wealthy man?"

🍺 🍺 🍺

"Fifty percent chance of rain. What does that mean?"

🍺 🍺 🍺

"Can flies fly upside-down? If not, how do they get on the ceiling?"

🍺 🍺 🍺

"In 1893 or so, there were thirteen cars in the U.S. and two cars hit head-on in Kansas City. How could that happen?"

🍺 🍺 🍺

Other

"Today I memorized all the numbers in the telephone book. Tomorrow, I'll start on the names."

"I can't forget names after taking that Sam Carnegie course." The Dale Carnegie, Dale not Sam, memory course was popular for many years.

When introduced to a person named Smith, Earl would ask if they ever thought of changing their name to Jones. Earl would do the same in reverse when introduced to someone named Jones.

If someone called out Earl's name or said, "hello Earl" he would say, "that's my name too."

"Before being drafted into the military during World War II, I was a factory worker at General Motors (GM). I quit GM after thirty-six months and twenty-two days in the Army Air Corp. If I would have stayed at GM, I could have been chairman of the board."

🍺 🍺 🍺

"I was born forty years too soon…or I need a bigger town."

🍺 🍺 🍺

"A guy asked me yesterday 'How are you doing?' I said, 'horrible' and he said, 'that's good.' No one gives a damn."

🍺 🍺 🍺

"We went to different schools together. I think we weren't friends."

🍺 🍺 🍺

"You sat in the last row and back seat. I was right behind you."

🍺 🍺 🍺

"High school today. No!"

🍺 🍺 🍺

"During the bad times we would jack-off the dogs to feed the cats. We had mean cats and happy dogs."

🍺 🍺 🍺

When shaking a kid's hand Earl would sometimes say, "You're a fart smeller. I mean smart fella."

🍺 🍺 🍺

"I takes ugly pills…and they work."

🍺 🍺 🍺

"If you're driving…be sure you've got your car."

🍺 🍺 🍺

"If you must ride in a plane, always sit as far back as possible. You never hear of a plane backing into a mountain."

🍺 🍺 🍺

CHAPTER 5
EARL'S ADVICE

"I've made a million mistakes and if I did it over, I would do the same things again."

"Sometimes you eat the bear, and sometimes the bear eats you."

"I can't solve your problems because I have enough of my own. But if you talk about your problems, you might be able to figure out solutions."

"You can't do anything about yesterday. Don't worry about it."

"Yesterday is gone, can't do nothing about it."

"Today is the first day of the rest of your life."

🍺 🍺 🍺

"You have to fix problems before they start."

🍺 🍺 🍺

"Stop them before they start."

🍺 🍺 🍺

"Everyone you meet is your superior in one way or another. Maybe they can drink more beer."

🍺 🍺 🍺

"The early bird gets the worm."

🍺 🍺 🍺

"People of good taste like nice things."

🍺 🍺 🍺

"They love you…you get anything you want…if you prove to them that you don't need it."

🍺 🍺 🍺

"The dog that shits fast, doesn't shit long."

🍺 🍺 🍺

"In the bar and most other places, you never discuss politics or religion."

🍺 🍺 🍺

Over the years Earl had countless customers that regularly visited him in his various bars. He always remembered their faces and what they drank, but sometimes he forgot a person's name. When this happened Earl would ask them their name. If they gave Earl a first name, he would tell them he knew that and ask for their last name. Obviously if Earl were given a last instead of a first name, his statement and question would be reversed. Earl might also say, "hello old buddy" if he recognized you but did not remember your name. Or "hello good people" if Earl saw a couple that he didn't know by name.

🍺 🍺 🍺

"When I first started bartending, I thought I couldn't be right, and all of these people are wrong. Fifty years later I was right."

🍺 🍺 🍺

"Do you know what the old Indian said? Fuck um."

🍺 🍺 🍺

"Money is not important…until you run out."

"I wish someone would have told me that money is important. I could've had a barrel full."

"There is not enough hours in the day to get rich, you have to make money while you sleep."

"You learn things behind a bar that they don't teach in college."

"A bartender knows when someone has had enough."

"I have a cigar box full of bad checks. They'll beat you and even die to do so."

"If your bartender is making $100 per week and needs $150, they will get it."

🍺 🍺 🍺

"Always get the money first." Earl told his son Dean this, while Dean was bartending for the first time, and he served a customer who quickly drank his beer and walked out without paying.

🍺 🍺 🍺

Doug Alger was playing pool, eight-ball, at Earl's Saloon and he won every game, beating a guy out of all of his cash plus $250. The guy said he was going to his car to get a check, but he never returned to the bar. Earl watched this happen, and thinking like a true gambler, told Doug that he should have let the guy win a few games, and also left a few dollars in his pocket, so the guy would come back sometime and play him again.

🍺 🍺 🍺

"Women are like streetcars. There's one on every corner."

🍺 🍺 🍺

"You lose weight when your calorie intake is less than your energy output."

🍺 🍺 🍺

"Overweight look at your watch, 8 A.M. time to eat, noon time to eat, 5 P.M. time to eat."

🍺 🍺 🍺

Earl told his grandchildren, "Use these four magic words to make your life simple: yes sir/ma'am, no sir/ma'am, please, and thank you."

🍺 🍺 🍺

Some grandchildren were also told, "Nothing good happens after midnight."

🍺 🍺 🍺

"If you get an education, no one can take it away from you."

🍺 🍺 🍺

"Get your education and change the world."

🍺 🍺 🍺

"The best advice I can give you is…finish school."

🍺 🍺 🍺

"If you buy a house, buy one on the water."

🍺 🍺 🍺

"Life's too short to smoke a cheap cigar."

🍺 🍺 🍺

"This country needs term limits (for members of Congress) to solve its problems."

🍺 🍺 🍺

"If they're in …vote them out."

🍺 🍺 🍺

"How old would you be if you didn't know how old you are?" Earl said this was the secret of living a long and happy life.

🍺 🍺 🍺

"The smartest man in the world, Ward Collins' grandpa, told us when we were kids 'Get it while you're young.'" Ward Collins and Earl were best friends while growing up together.

🍺 🍺 🍺

"At ninety-five years old, I'm not sure if it's better to die young or live to be an old man."

🍺 🍺 🍺

"God is good." Earl was baptized and born again late in life. His family and friends often heard him say and tell people that God is good.

🍺 🍺 🍺

John Gordon Smith stopped in Earl's bar and told Earl about all of the problems he was dealing with. As a joke Earl said, "If I was you, I would rob a bank and leave town." The next day Earl read in the local newspaper that his friend had robbed a bank and was arrested on his way out of town. The moral of this story is to be careful when you give someone advice.

🍺 🍺 🍺

Earl and June Waving Goodbye

EARL'S NOTES

I'm just a Dumb Bartender well say Peter

Fifteen yr old Nice Fairy gave me a choice of big Peter or a good memory. Which Did you Take.

I don't Remember

It's mine I can work it as fast as I want to ⊗

First drink tonite standing on my left foot right hand Facing S.W.

One Arm Fisherman
Don't drink water Fish swim in

Told Bouncer I get the bottle he might have a Knive

Late in life Him trouble wife ask what happen You use to jump over bar Throw them out door. Now you walk around and ask them to leave.

Work 15/hr day for 50 yr never late missed 1 or the day drank 2 Qt of Booze Smoked 2 oz Thos pk

I was going to be a Brain Surgeon But the Family wanted me to learn a Trade. So he became a Bar Tender

I started at a dollar an hour, Free drinks and a little strange stuff. Best Job I ever had.

① Beer you never own it. You just rent it

② It all comes out of the same horse

Jack Tilly New Car Dead Fish

Bartender hundred $ week if they need $150 They will get it

Waitress denied drinking said she had one every time I did

Bartender - Had a drink every time you did
If they didn't drink I could not use them

Stealing Gas. robbery Bank
~~Holding Tin foilers~~
Ashes on Table
~~50¢~~ ~~Quarters~~ in beer bottle 50¢ a Slice

Sam $100 yr bymt every Stig a Slice
Every 3 month Fingernail Falls off But always grows Back

— NEVER HIT A WOMAN
KILL HER.

Meet Couple goof customers
get married Places
Have Kids turn 21
Bring in meet Earl later
Kids get married own Kid
bring Kids In. Meet Earl
Been hre too long
June Doctor Cab driver
Take Blouse off

3 Pigs gun behind Bar

At my age 86 I don't buy
green Bananas (92 Coushing overtime)

Can't forget names after taking
Sam Carnige Course

B. Muller. See him in bar of People
Bob say Earl you ought to be Hung
I say I am I am
Drunk enough to keep small bar going

If No one shows up will still
do good Business

50 years. I told them if any
one he fought It had to be fair
and I can't whip my wife

STop them before they start
Knew all Thiefs &
Trouble Makers

First started Bartending
I thought Earl you couldn't
be right and all these people
wrong 50 yrs later I was right

Ⓧ Some Day 66 yrs last Oct
Ⓐ Tell girls you have to get
something Straight between you

Least Tip I got were 2nd. Jet toddy
1st Horse Rad.
How to win worried lucky of Cheat
Two Bad habits
Smoking & Sleep
Check - West Bank of Miss
Cigar Box full checks.
Beat you if They have to die

Long John Silver — eye, leg, arm
Waitress sitting on a million dollars

Can Flies Fly upside down?
How do they get on ceiling?

Fella asked me yesterday
How are you doing I said
Horrible, He said Thats good
No One gives a damn

I drink Vodka I make
Your Peter grow

---

6 P EARL Firstname
2 Waitresses Otherside
Wayne Taafe's Table
Tape recorder

Can't Forget name
Sam C.

Meet Smith or Jones
ask them if they ever
Thought about changing
names to other

Twins FirstMeet ask if they
are They Still Bro. or Sister

How to Spell Whiskey,
Single girls Jealous People

Forty yrs ago Bro in Law D A.
Knew all Police Could have
shot 6 people Police tell me
go home if needed they call
Excuse Police hear my Story
I go and let you stay open

Before being drafted I went to
work for G.M. Quit after
36 months and 27 days in
the army. If I had stayed
I might have been Chairman
of the board.

Give away
Peter & Bubble Gum out

Mom said call me a Cab
Your a Cab

Waitress had Two chances to get
Pregnant. She blew Both of them

Knee Trouble Left Knee OK Rt Knee D A
Trouble with Wee Knee

---

15 Hrs Day 2 QT 3 Pks Cig.
Never Drink Water Fish Swim
Doug Davis - Tequila Lemon QT.
Pin Note on Drunk Cab.

Die tomorrow No big deal.
Nursing Home Bad.

Scout. How old would you be
Dad died 59 old · He was old man
↑ Turkey in raffle
Colored man to funeral How Baby Well

Dave Horoscope
                    Back Viet
Dave - Late - 30 min. early
4 Kids in College
        same time
High School today No

My Wife run away with
my best Friend and I
miss him

Wife takes Ugly Pills and they work

June - Washington DC

Diet Pills (Ole Yellow) $100
⊕ up at lakes throw to duck
all night Quack Quack Quack
swimming in Circle

Jonsey bar Play Browan
2 Bro + Wife
    Fight

Jeff Hardin   John
               Pall
               bearer

⊗ Lose Weight
   Calories intake less than
   Energy out Put.

Pallbearers should Change
out hired 4 Cait wait Jeff
Big names.

       Judge if I go to court
⊗ want Judge to know my
   name   Simon Dross Regis

Higginbottom says word 4 Cove 2/6 Pk
after 66 yr married
Sex in nice when going to bed
" in nice in the morning
But sometime don't think of
        Manitre

Doug Davis drink on way
to operation / Tequila
Big Bill - Where did you meet
                      them

Jerry Hite wrong Shift

Money Not Important.
I've got enough to last
me the rest of my life.
If I die before Midnight.

Not Important till you
Run out.

Bill Dave Ben.

Told Grand Kids 4 Magic words to
make life simple
1. Yes Sir
2. No Sir
3. Thank you
4. Please

---

3 Mistakes   1. Voting
             2. Drinking
   Women   3. Bar

All of a sudden I'm getting up
The same time I got in for 50 yrs

Don't you want to own
a Hotel?

Every one you meet is your
Superior in one way or other

Maybe he can drink more Beer

Made 1 million mistakes do over
same ones again.

Wish someone told me money was
Important could have had barrel

My First By tender Job / Tank Wash
filler own $5   Beer 25¢ Whey 55¢   after 30
day saw him Told him I was going to
beat his butt next time saw him
He said we will be even then
Told him to Forget it

Check for Blue Cross
If you tear one they can sue you

Flying Sit in back of Plane

If you are driving
be sure you got your Car
Went to Hawaii But asked if I
Fly. No I drove

Can't solve your Problems
Have Trouble with mine
Get you thinking you OK

got home every morning door
locked. Had Donuts for Kids
already gone to school.

All # in Telephone book
Tomorrow start on names.

Today First Day of Rest of your life
Can't do anything about yesterday
Don't worry about

Easy Job. Weatherman.
50% chance of Rain
What does that mean?
Jim Save her life
Check her for Breast cancer
every morning ⊗

Screws in head Losse
Walk up ask if he
Still likes Boys. Yes
Help Earl get to Hawaii get Back
Ask Name Know that one I mean
last or First name

⊗ If you own Bank $1000 they
own you. But if you own
them $50,000 you own them

⊗ They loan you anything you want
If you prove to them you don't need it

Secret Getting Old
How old would you be
⊗ If you didn't know how old you

1st T shirt I am a virgin
on Back this is a old shirt
I am 89 counting overtime
Told Waitress take day off go get strong
Gone for Three days to go went
Indianapolis

Vegas Caesars Palace Mirror
over dressed 3 nite clothes off
waiting for Beer
Vegas manager Wouldn't need #1 for Beer
Dang. moved 17 times in 22 yrs.
Wife thinks I started WW 2 ⊗
Yesterday is gone Can't do
nothing about it. ⊗

Smartest Man in world.
⊗ Ward Collins Grand Papa
Get it while you are young
Too Drunk to walk

all people in this book are
innocent until proving guilty
if they are still in Town
| Earl | Friends | Bartenders | Enemies | By Name |
| Family | | Waitress | | |

- Clinton could have been Worse
- He could have been Homo —

- Lesbians aren't bad They like Girls
- So do I.
- Didn't find out diffrence between Boys + Girls Till I got married. Never stepped out. I am sort like a Wiggin

---

- Stomach no much no more mind fill I four Ears
- Over weight look at weight 12:00 Time to eat 5" Limit eat
- Ind Univ. wants my Liver

Juke Box New Elvis
Don't let your Meat Loaf and
It was South of the Border But She Still came across
Put down change for $10 Ask him if it was $5 or $10 Real Quick say $10
It was $20 if they are drunk

---

100 Customs never had $100
Some day buying Bar want me to run it.
Ind Univ. wants my Liver

1893 (?) 13 cars in U.S.
Two must head on in Kans City
Minty McClure 25 times Nursing Home 11 yrs
Had it won Loose last 27 fights

Why More House Asses then
Horses Title?
Born Twenty years too Soon or Bigger Town
Bartender Tell End make me check my gun
40 years ago Every one had gun but me

You sat in last row back seat
I was just behind you School
Went to diffrent schools Together Think we werent Friends.

One Arm fisherman
Pall Bearers
Geo Grunwell $100 loan
I Came back called me Carl

Katy Did   Katy Will
H. Lunsford   Don't feel like Drinking
Tape Recorder   Wayne Stables
Stables Redmond Don't like you
Allen Check dinner leaves Tip

6 Hamburger 25¢
15¢ a day lunch
$5 all nite go home change
knew real quick Ham, C Bays, Ham,
Quit G.M. 35 wk · made 75 - 100 hrs
Donuts 33¢ doz   now 50 each
Coneys 10 for a dollar
Pepsi Cola 25¢ hour

Oysters half shell   only 10 worked
Drunk call wife come get him
He in showers. Come get him when done
First Time free charge second time
Knock on front Door run around back
Twenty dollars on dresser

Ed. H buying dog shots
D.H. Ind. Supreme Court Justice
I suppose if you birthday too
have a drink
Dave going to law School.
Good visiting D.A. meeting X gov.
Lic. Plate no police man Tio

Leo Cambell broken Leg Drink
Stables   Rooms & bath
no Rent
Didn't have Key Running Hor House
Shoot out People Police - go Home

Tom Hock meeting him
Ed Ward OK with you
   add People
some in bar
Hated to see them until I had
a couple of drinks OK then

Tom Busby

Ron Clark bet Pendleton 25 pts $5
although bet $5 Pendleton didn't show
   Broke even
Joe Eddie ahead 3 $50 games Charles
lent me $50 he win next 3 games
Bill Cokin Elks Mgr ahead all
check go have breakfast he come
to house to book 500
Pony Express Molly Beaver Jail

Jim Ditzer Sailboat
B. Glazier wanting to
help me Call this wife
B Glazier Buy 1½ Sell 2½

Shannon Best handicapper in Town
Lost more money then anyone
~~that~~ Ward Davis Trainer
in Ohio Bet horse Jockey
fell off.

Horse pull Ice Wagon
Shit in street,   Tom
Harry Taylor Bookie (1st Bet)

---

4 MAGIC WORDS
      FOR TEENS
YES SIR   NO SIR
THANK YOU   PLEASE
GOT YOU EDUCATION
CHANGE THE WORLD

SAVE JUNE'S LIFE
EVERY MORN. CHECK
HER FOR BREAST C

1st married Mowed yard
~~June didn't like it~~
T.S. Birthday Radio, T.V.
Airplane Newspaper
Bottle of Vodka

X Early Bird - Worm
Dan Patch race.
X Cancer Causes Smoking
This Summer + Night
Quit when I got back M ici
all size of Roosters
George Rainbo still like boys

Best you ever did to it
Shoes in Reach In.
Jim Cancer hospital Florida
Wrong end of spoon
X Why walk when Ride to Piece
Im not along to get hat
                          with

WOMEN 3 MISTAKES
1 LET THEM VOTE
2 LET DRIVE CAR
3 LEV I TAVERNS

Yrs ago when I was a kid and I was tall and good looking. Now I am 86 yrs old and old and fat. I did a lot of fighting Golden Gloves until I had trouble with my hands. The Referee kept stepping on them.

In high school I was too small for most sports, but I was good at two of them. I was a broad jumper and a Javelin catcher. You would throw the Javelin and then run and catch it.

Been married 67 yrs last Oct. When I first got married I mowed the yard. Wife very choosey about her yard and house. She didn't like the way I mowed it. 66 yrs later she wont let me do it again. For sixty yrs she has complained about my smoking. For yrs. I got away with it by telling her I was going to smoke this yr. and next. She finaly wised up. So I told her I was going to quit.

When I got back from Mich. she said we are going to Mich. I said were not

---

Bill Radford Fulmer
Doc Woods 1up Love Chu hutts
Swimming Pool Cashing Check Dom
wrong end of Spoon

Bear is sock broken on head
Make me one just a lil
White 10" and white nothing Black

Mr Boston Book Fri nite used them
Fred Spencer
Nown Held Ballgames
Horse Radish Police
God Damn Email

First Joke ever told Ⓧ
Brain Surgeon lawn mower
Stag Movies Falling g love
Selling Shoes
Low Tomunner Stupidly
Way over there
Paul Wilson
John Smith Bank
Judge knows my name
Venden Redman Indon

DON'T CHASE SINGLE
GIRL. THEY GOT
JEALOUS BOY FRIEND
GET A MARRIED WOMAN

Judge S. Cig paper smoke
Judge S Birthday Party.
Paul Green. Coal Shuttle

Fred Chon futh
Iwouldn't fire
Fox Jumps Tomorrow
2 Waitress on defford Silver(plant)
Adam + Eve
Long Put in nickel
Take out Dime
Saw This Place is
all new

Bob Church. Jail
Don Works.
Eggs Butter Milk Che
Waitress. at By D
Swimming Pool at Fort Lou
Phone Calls call Doc Wool
1 ot bring to get hand
out
Sim Carney cousin
Can't forget name

Think no, between 1 to 10 you Love
Take Clothes off.
1st time is Free 2nd Time I get to change up
Check Blue Cross. Take what you want don't
hurt yourself.
Shoes in Kooler for 6 PK
Ed Hedgepeth. buying a fifth of whiskey
Judge S. Vodka present ½

Made in the USA
Columbia, SC
29 November 2023

07ef1323-d908-4d24-bcf2-a2849bfa9cf1R01